WATERWAYS

UNIVERSITY PRESS OF FLORIDA

Florida A&M University, Tallahassee
Florida Atlantic University, Boca Raton
Florida Gulf Coast University, Ft. Myers
Florida International University, Miami
Florida State University, Tallahassee
New College of Florida, Sarasota
University of Central Florida, Orlando
University of Florida, Gainesville
University of North Florida, Jacksonville
University of South Florida, Tampa
University of West Florida, Pensacola

Jennifer Frick-Ruppert

Waterways

Sailing the
Southeastern Coast

UNIVERSITY PRESS OF FLORIDA

Gainesville · Tallahassee · Tampa

Boca Raton · Pensacola · Orlando

Miami · Jacksonville · Ft. Myers · Sarasota

University Press of Florida
15 Northwest 15th Street
Gainesville, FL 32611-2079
http://www.upf.com

To Ed,
who traveled every mile and edited every word,
and to Fritz,
who has recently come along for the ride

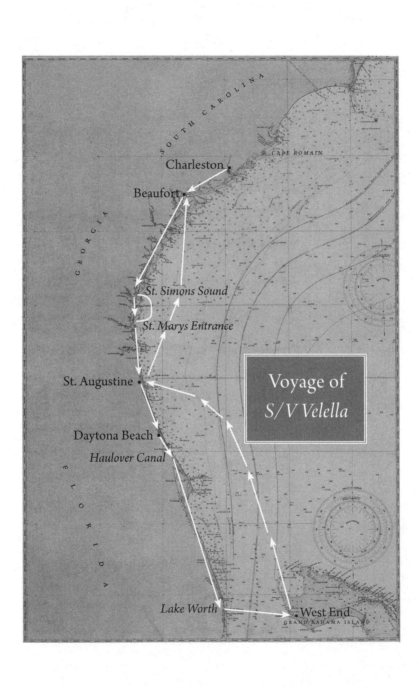

Charleston

Beaufort

St. Simons Sound

St. Marys Entrance

St. Augustine

Daytona Beach

Haulover Canal

Lake Worth

West End
GRAND BAHAMA ISLAND

SOUTH CAROLINA

CAPE ROMAIN

GEORGIA

FLORIDA

Voyage of
S/V Velella

Contents

Preface

I am a biologist-naturalist and a sailor, and if you enjoy either natural history or sailing, I hope that you will find this book entertaining. My husband and I have sailed in the waters and among the marshes, mudflats, and sandbanks of North Carolina, South Carolina, Georgia, Florida, and the Bahamas for nearly twenty years. This book is chiefly a rhapsody on nature, although it is also a record of some challenges, now humorous in retrospect, we encountered as novice sailors. At its heart, however, it is a tribute to the plants and animals—spartina, blue crabs, skimmers, dolphins, sand dollars, and spot-tailed bass, to name but a few—that live and prosper in the swift waters and dynamic landforms of the coastal Southeast.

An appreciation of the nature of creeks, salt marshes, mudflats, sand banks, and the open sea requires commitment and fortitude, especially aboard a non-air-conditioned sailboat at the height of a southeastern summer, but the reward is an immersion in the wonders of nature. The typical speed of sailing, hardly faster than walking, is the ideal pace for observing nature—slow enough to see all, fast enough to avoid boredom. The cruise I describe in this book was such a voyage, an adventure of discovery. It was our first passage, when everything we saw and experienced was totally new, often unexpected, and sometimes an effort to integrate into our perception of ourselves.

I should also clarify that this book is not a novel or memoir, with a focus on character development. My husband and I were certainly transformed as we learned to sail and to study coastal nature, but the real story is nature herself: the interaction of sea and land, the teeming thousands of fantastic animals that occupy a sandy beach, or the flight of birds before a rainstorm. I became a more confident sailor as we cruised through marshes and inlets and offshore waters, and I became a better person, too, more aware of my surroundings, my effect on others, my place in the natural world, part of a larger whole rather than its center.

These changes in attitude resulted from our voyage afloat. To be immersed in nature is humbling, but also empowering because you are called upon to do your best with whatever is offered—a storm, a grounding, wind, waves—none of which can be controlled, but all of which a boater must react to appropriately.

Through it all, the one constant is change. The water flows in one direction and then reverses, a shoal grows out from one side of a channel while the other side erodes, some shrimp are caught and eaten while others survive to reproduce. Simply by paying attention to the vicissitudes of nature, by acknowledging the variation around us, we ourselves are transformed. And while much of the change we observe is evenly balanced between loss and gain, we also find examples in which one entity benefits disproportionately at the expense of another, and we wonder, as exploitation becomes more commonplace, if we are witnessing incomprehensible losses.

But nature is ever beautiful and remarkably resilient. While sailing in North Carolina's Pamlico Sound, our current cruising ground, I can imagine how it must have seemed to the first English explorers who sailed in and met the Natives already living here. The composition of plants, animals, and humans is not the same as it was then, but it is still complex, picturesque, and culturally unique. The fish aren't as large or as numerous, the water is more murky, the tribes of Native peoples reduced, but you can still be the only boat on the water, reel in a flounder big enough to keep, and get caught in a thunderstorm whose ferocity takes away your breath. While one is afloat in a small boat upon the water, at the mercy of wind, waves, and sandbars, nature is close and alive with power and beauty.

Waterways celebrates this natural beauty. It is about sailing and nature, wonder and beauty, joy and pleasure, all there for you when you step aboard, cast off the lines, and sail away from the dock. Come along.

Introduction

WHILE I RELEASE THE DOCKING LINES, ED SLOWLY EDGES *Velella* out into the river's current. We let the current take us, drifting gently toward the sea while we stow the docking lines and loose the sails. To stow those lines, to shove them back into the darkness of the hold, is the final satisfying release from the land and our lives there. Here in the river, we begin anew.

Sailing is a departure from the hustle of the world. It is a sort of forced meditation on nature. Mostly a sailboat moves slowly, propelled only by moving air, and this deliberate but dreamlike motion enhances each experience. When a sailboat moves quickly, motion itself becomes foremost as senses fill with the rush of perfumed wind past billowing sails, the creaks and groans of strained rigging, and salty spray flying up from the water bubbling along the bow. Whitman, a sailor, too, recognized this sense of motion and movement, describing it as:

> Below, a myriad myriad waves hastening, lifting up their necks,
> Tending in ceaseless flow toward the track of the ship,
> Waves of the ocean bubbling and gurgling, blithely prying,
> Waves, undulating waves, liquid, uneven, emulous waves.

As in a dream, sailing changes your sense of space and motion. A full day lived outdoors and a night filled with the sounds of wind, water, and fellow creatures just on the other side of the hull loosen the bonds of convention and awaken us from the slumber of everyday living. On the water, a gentle swell transforms the boat into a rocking cradle, but the stability of land can be sickeningly under-mined by the pitching, rolling, and yawing of the boat through a confused sea. Even the walls of your waterborne home may stand at a nightmarish angle as the boat heels to the wind.

To live in such a changeable situation requires accommodation, an easing of expectations, a re-creation of self. Constant change re-quires reflection, evaluation, and adjustment. Once embraced, the rhythm of waves and tides and cycles of sun and moon become second nature, and a deep resonance is discovered between these movements and the harmony of body and being.

Sailors are compelled to live in tiny, though often elegant, accom-modations and adopt a strict economy. For most sailors, their boat's entire living area is smaller than that of a single room in an average house yet it contains all that is essential for a comfortable life. There is no room for excess because the fundamentals associated with food, water, and shelter occupy the limited space. But the reward for cramped accommodations is the liberty to pursue a boundless hori-zon with the world at your doorstep. It is as if space expands in pro-portion to your detachment from encumbrances. As a result, sailing your little ship over an expanse of water conveys a profound sense of freedom and self-reliance. You might be the only warm spark in the cosmos.

Sailing is also like time travel. It provides a connection to an earlier epoch before machines powered by fossil fuels industrial-ized the world and put time at a premium. It is a reminder that the way we live today, with our society's intense focus on energy and consumption, is a relatively recent phenomenon to which we are only awkwardly and often uncomfortably adapted. When we step aboard our sailboat and hoist sails instead of turning a key to crank an engine, we step onto an ark that connects us both physically and mentally with a bygone era when the world was unpolluted by the wastes from fossil fuels and much less crowded with civilization. It also promises, as did embarking on Noah's boat, a new beginning, in this case one that embraces renewable energy, reduced consumption, and appreciation of biodiversity.

The pace of a boat under sail is, by contemporary standards of travel, slow, roughly in the range of walking to ordinary bicycling. It is not a preferred mode of travel for anyone with arrival-time anxiety. But for many, deceleration is exactly the therapy needed. This slower pace allows the time to observe and contemplate not only the general land- or seascape passing by, but also the fine details and rich textures of the natural world. Slow travel attaches the traveler to nature, freeing us to explore life and embrace every moment as if it is the only one that matters. In this sense, sailing heightens awareness, raises consciousness, and in uniting us with nature, satisfies a deep primordial longing.

Marshes are the heart of the southeastern coast. They teem with life and are nearly uninhabited by humanity. Their rhythm beats at a pace that differs from that of offices and deadlines. The vast uniformity of salt marsh, like that of prairie grasslands or waves breaking endlessly on the strand, conveys a feeling of order and serenity unrealizable in the crush of crowds. As biologists and naturalists, the opportunity to observe and learn from southeastern salt marshes while living and cruising aboard a sailboat draws us like moths to a light.

Velella, our vehicle of exploration and our home, is a traditionally designed, thirty-seven-foot Tayana sailboat. Her cutter rig, with three sails and a single mast, is easy to handle and provides options for sail combinations. We also outfitted her with a colorful cruising spinnaker, or "nylon diesel," to be used in light wind or when sailing with wind directly over the stern. Because the spinnaker boasts as much area as the other three sails combined, it propels the boat much like a diesel engine but without the fuel. We do have an engine, and find it invaluable for maneuvering in tight spaces, docking, and moving when there is no wind, but we sail as often as possible.

Velella can take us anywhere on the globe that water touches. She is built to perform under rough sailing conditions, and is steady enough to pull us through them. As a heavy displacement vessel designed for open-ocean, blue-water sailing, she is not easily knocked about by high winds and waves. Her full keel and canoe stern allow her to handle a following sea gracefully, riding gently up over the waves.

She is roomy inside, with a comfortable main cabin. A galley with sink and stove opens to the left, or port side of the entry, called the companionway, and a navigation station and single quarter-berth opens to starboard. Located forward of the main cabin, the head consists of a sink, toilet, and shower, and the V-berth occupies the bow. We sleep in the V-berth, our feet in the narrow end and shoulders occupying the wider part of the V.

Although the head is tiny, it is a vast improvement over an original. At the very front, or head, of historical oceangoing ships, open wooden grates flank the bowsprit, a spar that projects forward like a unicorn's horn and from which the forward sails are flown. Sailors walked out onto these grates and held onto rope lines when they needed to "use the head." During rough weather, waves washed the heads and sailors used "honey-buckets" in their cabins instead, whose contents they then had to fling downwind and overboard.

Velella's exterior is covered with wood. She sports a spruce mast and boom, teak decks, and a solid-teak bowsprit that projects forward from the bow. The cabin trim, caprails, blocks, and bulwarks are all teak, and each set of steel shrouds supports a teak pinrail to hold lines and teak lightboard to hold brass kerosene lights. All of the wood is finished in high-gloss varnish, except for the decks, which are left natural. Although the hull is fiberglass, its pattern of board-like grooves makes it appear to be wooden as well. The hull is so well made that it lacks a single blister or delamination, and when the sun is low on the horizon, sunlight diffuses through the fiberglass to light up the cabin interior. The first time we noticed this rather disconcerting light transmission, we assumed that the hull must be awfully thin to allow light to pass through it, but soon learned that the phenomenon indicated high-quality fiberglass. Even though it is logical that good glass fibers should conduct light, it did seem counterintuitive that a strong, well-built boat would do so.

In keeping with tradition, her deck hardware is almost all bronze, its pinkish-brown color perfectly complementing the honeyed teak. Four bronze dorade vents perch atop their teak boxes on the cabin-top, each ingeniously designed to allow air but prevent water flow into the interior cabin, and the heavy bronze winches and cleats are backed by teak blocks. On the forward-most part of the cabintop, a wooden hatch opens into the master V-berth down below, and just behind the mast a second hatch opens into the main cabin. Instead of opening forward, it opens from the midline of the boat toward each side, the same way that a butterfly flaps its wings.

To us the bronze touches are a pleasant connection to sailing's history. Bronze was historically used aboard ships because it resists the corrosive action of seawater. Carbon-steel or iron must be "parceled and served"—tightly wound with fabric and then sealed with tar to protect it from salt and water. Since the manufacture of stainless steel, which resists seawater corrosion, it has become the most frequently used metal aboard ships. While bronze requires polishing to keep it in shiny condition and stainless steel does not, bronze has an advantage over stainless in addition to its earthy beauty. When stainless steel eventually succumbs to corrosion and wear, it breaks, cracking along a line of shear. Bronze does not because it resists metal fatigue. With stainless steel shrouds and stays supporting Velella's mast, we make an annual trip to her mast-top to check specifically for dangerous hairline fractures in the attachment plates, but our bronze hardware does not require the same degree of evaluation. It just needs elbow grease and polish.

Inside Velella's cabin, the ambiance is like that of Henry Higgins's library. From railings to cabinet fronts, drawers and shelves, all is delicately carved teak. The care and pride with which she was constructed are evident in each rounded corner and perfectly joined joint. The Taiwanese boatyard that built her hired whole families to live aboard while they completed the internal work. Since the boat was home, and the family was responsible for its appearance, the quality of their work was uncompromised. While we are the beneficiaries of that care, we are also its connoisseurs. Artisans may work without ever receiving the direct acknowledgment of the quality of their work, yet their skill and effort is appreciated and admired half a world away.

We fell in love with *Velella* immediately, recognizing her as our boat. Not only is she strong enough for making offshore passages, but she is comfortable for us to live aboard for weeks at a time. Her pretty wood and bronze accents connect us to history and to biology, for that teak bowsprit and spruce mast came from forests of trees in different parts of the world. Teak wood, from tropical rainforests, is rot resistant and therefore used aboard ships for decking and cabin trim. Spruce is used for the mast because it is straight, strong, and lightweight, and the trees are conifers that grow in Canadian and other boreal forests. In colonial times, spruce and pine trees large and straight enough to become ship masts were so important that they were marked with "the King's cross," which designated them solely for British shipping and created conflict with the Americans who wanted them for other uses.

This is the story of our first summer cruise, from Charleston, South Carolina, through Georgia and Florida, across to the Bahamas, and back to Beaufort, South Carolina. The dreams of sailing, warmth, and escape from the routine and cold of winter are transformed into reality as we loosen the docking lines and sail into the marshes. Some new sight inevitably appears, no matter how many times we travel the same path and, most of all, we connect to nature, to each other, and to ourselves. While most other cruisers search for cooler weather and head north in summertime, we run counter to the usual current and point our bow south, into the marshes and beyond. These, then, are our songs of the salt marsh, rhapsodies on the sea, and of learning to see while learning to sail. Come with us on a waterway voyage.

Charleston to Beaufort

AHEAD OF THE BOW STRETCHES AN ENDLESS, GREEN SEA OF marsh grass with a narrow thread of dark water weaving through it. That slender meander of water is the Intracoastal Waterway, or ICW, which runs like a vein through the tidal marshes. It will carry us from Charleston to Beaufort, an easy daylong trip in what we hope will be a nice introduction to voyaging on the waterway.

In all this vast expanse of marsh, a single plant is the overwhelmingly dominant species. It is called *Spartina alterniflora*, marsh grass, cordgrass, or just spartina. Its habitat is harsh, yet it thrives nonetheless. Covered by salt water twice each day, then completely dried out and exposed to the sun at least once, it is inexorably tied to the rhythm of tides. After a summer thunderstorm, marsh grass glows in the fresh green of rain-washed new growth, and as the breeze plays through the leaves of grass, dancing droplets sparkle like diamonds among the blades as sunlight strikes them. As A. R. Ammons describes in his poem "Small Song": "The reeds give/way to the/wind and give/the wind away."

We depart from our Charleston marina in early morning, soon after the sun breaks the river's surface, the docks dewy from cool night air. With nocturnal animals now silent and diurnal animals barely awake, only a few boat-tailed grackles, with raucous, tinny calls, stir about. The marsh smells sweet, cleaned from last night's high tide. A few puffy clouds hold some pink from the sunrise.

I smile at Ed as I coil up docking lines and take in fenders. He stands at the helm, hands gripped gently around the gleaming wooden wheel. We both wear jackets because the air is cool and damp on this early May morning, the month of coastal South Carolina's transition between spring's wide temperature swings and the constant heat of summer.

"What would you like to see this morning, Jennifer?" Ed calls up toward me, as I walk back along the deck to the cockpit, fenders and lines in hand to stow away in the cockpit locker.

"I do believe I'd like to see some marsh grass!" I respond. "Know where I can find any?" He chuckles because there are literally hundreds of acres of salt marsh stretched out on either side of us. "You know," I say to Ed, "one thing I haven't seen before is a real *Velella* even though we named our boat after such a creature. Suppose we will see one when we get to Florida?"

When we acquired *Velella*, she was called something strange that was a garbled compilation of the names of the former owner's family. Within a few days of finalizing her purchase, I perched in a rocking dinghy tied off beside her and began removing the old name from the stern by heating the vinyl letters with a hair-dryer. After peeling them off, I scrubbed her clean and measured out the placement for stencils of her new name, V-e-l-e-l-l-a. I feel sure that she was *Velella* all along, but needed us to recognize her true identity.

Before I could completely apply the name to the starboard side, a nearby boater began to study the letters, and as I erased the final marks of alignment and leaned back in the dinghy to evaluate my work, he began to walk up the dock toward us. As he neared the boat, he looked with a critical eye first at the name, then at me, then back at the name. I waited, curiously; the placement was correct, level and even, no wrinkles. I whispered to *Velella*, "What is he evaluating? You look good to me!" Finally he seemed to make up his mind, stepped forward, and asked very slowly and loudly, "Is that *your* name?"

"What is this guy thinking," I wondered to myself, "*my* name?" But then I began to consider the situation as he saw it: a young woman, long black braid dangling down a back tanned a deep, almost teak-colored brown, working steadily on a Latin-named sailboat designed and built for long ocean passages. He nearly fell off the dock when I spoke, not with the Italian or Spanish accent he expected, but with an accent unmistakably of a child of the southeastern United States.

Velella is the name of an animal of the sea. A biologist with an aesthetic sense gave the scientific name *Velella velella* to a small creature commonly called "by-the-wind-sailor." ("Velum" is the Latin word for sail.) It resembles a miniature Portuguese man-o'-war and is composed of a two-inch-long, floating, oblong disk with a sail of living tissue set at an angle across it. These tiny yachts sail only downwind, but at an angle of 45 to 60 degrees to the wind direction, and some set their sails to port and some to starboard. Muscles in the sail allow them to extend it to increase sail area or shorten it the way we reef our mainsail to avoid capsizing in high wind. Hanging into the water are dozens of tentacles to capture food and several mouths to swallow it. Like its larger cousin, it is beautifully colored in gentle hues of blue, pink, and purple, but *V. velella* is small, its disk only a couple of inches in diameter with tentacles a few inches longer, and its sting is undetectable. *Velella* occurs worldwide in warm oceans, but usually far out at sea; however, when the predominant wind direction shifts, mass stranding on beaches may occur.

Jellies in general are among the most ancient animal forms on Earth. Circular fossils in the rocks of the Ediacaran hills of Australia, between 540 and 635 million years old, have been interpreted as cnidarians, the animal group to which the jellies and polyps such as coral, anemones, and *Velella* belong. Cnidae (pronounced with a silent *c*) are the stinging threads that the animals fire into the bodies of their prey or attackers. Animals like *Velella* have been drifting though

Earth's seas while fish developed backbones and then jaws, while amphibians crawled sluggishly out of the water onto land, while dinosaurs ranged across continents, when birds leaped into flight, and when a tiny shrew-like mammal stumbled out into a world of dying dinosaurs. Jellies and polyps were already ancient when the first human controlled fire, carved a spear, built a boat, hoisted a sail, and powered an engine by gasoline. Humanity's time on Earth is a blink compared to eons that *Velella's* relatives have floated through the changing sea. While Carl Sagan used the delicate, wind-catching form of a dandelion seed on which to base his imaginary spaceship in his book and television series *Cosmos*, he might just as easily have used the body shape of a cnidarian, an animal that has drifted through a span of unimaginable time on planet Earth.

We named *Velella's* dinghy *Chrysomitra*, which is one name given to *Velella's* minute offspring. Thousands are released by the adult in an armada of living dinghies. Because the tiny jelly and the larger form look different from one another, for many years it was assumed that they were different animals, but they are actually just different stages in the life of the same species. Fooled by such appearances, early biologists named each life stage including the earliest (*Conaria*), providing Garstang's couplet: "With an air-filled float and sail aslant upon a sparkling sea/*Conaria* merged her little stock in *Velella*, L.t.d.!"

Not only does *Velella's* name remind us of the immensity of time that animals of the sea represent, but her sails link us to the historical period of human exploration. While we have the luxury of motoring when the creeks are too narrow to easily sail, previous explorers relied solely on their sails or oars. Aboard *Velella*, we hearken back to a time of a much smaller human population, when the Southeast was occupied by tribes of Native Americans, and Europeans were making initial explorations of other continents in their sailing ships. War, devastating diseases, and slavery followed on their heels, changing landscapes and the lives of the Natives profoundly. Once we began to burn fossil fuels in engines, our population began to grow exponentially, as did our problems of pollution and resource exploitation. Some of the most significant changes in the landscape have occurred in only the last 150 years. Compared *to Velella's* long life on Earth, that time is incredibly brief, yet the changes we have wrought are profound.

At first I thought it surprising that boat owners refer to their boats with a feminine pronoun. It didn't take long, however, to realize that *Velella* definitely has a personality, and a feminine one at that. It may have been the way she took care of us through storms or waited patiently as a mother with a child while we learned how to sail. Perhaps it was her beauty, for when freshly varnished and painted, she could have won any pageant she entered. It may have been her large, round belly and transom, a giant version of the primitive statues of mother-goddesses, or our complete dependence on her when sailing, a tiny Mother Earth ship to support our lives. In any case, we call *Velella* "she," and always greet her, then wish her luck on parting. She is a true friend.

Navigating the ICW between Charleston and Beaufort is a new experience for us, since our initial sails in Charleston Harbor required only limited understanding of navigational markers. There, markers warned of shallow water, but we learned them as individual marks to watch for, not as an orderly system of channel markers.

The entire ICW, however, is marked by navigational aids. Since our bow points south, we keep the triangular, red markers to the left of the boat and the square, green markers to the right. Inlets, including Charleston Harbor, have a unique marker system designated as "Red Right Returning." Because the conflict between ICW markers and sea buoys can be confusing, yellow squares or triangles have been added to each ICW mark to clarify that the marker is part of the ICW system.

While Ed falls naturally into the role as helmsman, I just as easily slip into navigation. *Velella*, of course, is the powerhouse of the trio.

Since we are on the first day of our cruise, I am especially vigilant. As soon as we pass one ICW marker, I search for the next, using binoculars if the marks are too far away to see easily. Charts lie on deck beside me as I compare charts to the markers we pass.

Ospreys are unconcerned by green or red, it seems, for I see equal numbers of their nests on both sides of the channel. The birds appropriate channel markers as nesting platforms, and wide-eyed, fuzzy chicks stare out at us as we pass their aerie. As we approach a nest on one of Brickyard Creek's many markers, two adults startle us by screaming overhead as they hover nervously about their nest of young.

Pesticide residues severely affected ospreys, but their populations recovered once DDT, in particular, was banned from use in the United States. DDT poses two major problems. First is its propensity for biomagnification by the food chain, which leads to high levels in predators such as fish-eating birds. Although water may have extremely low levels of DDT, the microscopic, planktonic plants and animals concentrate the poison in their bodies, where it lodges and stays in their tissues. As plankters are consumed by minnows, the small fish concentrate even higher levels of DDT in their tissues. Larger fish, in turn, eat thousands of minnows over their lifetime, and each minnow contains a store of poison. The larger fish, therefore, accumulate larger doses. At each step of the food chain, the concentration of DDT in the tissues of the animal increases, until top predators, such as ospreys, contain enough DDT in their tissues to poison them. DDT is slow to degrade, which is why it is such an effective pesticide and why it stays within the body.

DDT and other persistent pollutants were the subjects of Rachel Carson's famous book *Silent Spring*. Its title suggests that songbirds, high up on the food chain, were being poisoned by chemicals used to kill insects lower on the food chain and their food source. Poisoning insects in our fields and forests also poisoned birds, and once they were gone, our spring mornings would be silent of birdsong.

Rachel Carson was also a marine biologist and wrote several other books about sea life. A coastal reserve, named in her honor, was established in Beaufort, North Carolina, across from the town and the Duke Marine Laboratory where she conducted research.

In Carson's time, we came to understand biomagnification, but now we know even more about these pesticides. To make things worse, DDT is an estrogen mimic—its chemical structure is similar enough to the hormone estrogen that an animal's body reacts as if it is absorbing quantities of this feminizing hormone. One of the side effects is thinning of eggshells so that when the parent bird settles on eggs to incubate them, they break and the embryo dies. But the primary problem of estrogen mimics in all animals, not just birds, is the feminization of males. Famously, the population of alligators in Lake Apopka in Florida was so severely affected by a spill of DDT and other chemical compounds that males hatched shortly after the spill were permanently unable to reproduce. In 2006, the *entire* population of male smallmouth bass from the Potomac River had eggs in their gonads. There are many other examples of male feminization.

Although DDT is no longer used in this country, it is still used elsewhere in the world and is transported over great distances by wind, water, and movement of animals. DDT has even been found in Antarctic snow and seabirds. Fifty years after application to a field, only half the DDT has broken down into other compounds. The pollutants pass through food chains without decomposing and are therefore transported around the whole world.

Moreover, estrogen mimics are found in various plastic compounds that are ubiquitous in our current society, and human reproduction and development have been affected. Starting in 1999, the Centers for Disease Control in Atlanta, Georgia, began testing human subjects every other year for known pollutants, reporting them in the *National Report of Human Exposure to Environmental Chemicals*. While lead has been declining in human populations, newer chemicals have been increasing, and scientists found residues in every human subject they tested, from newborns to octogenarians. We all carry measurable amounts of pesticide and plasticizer residues in our bodies.

Phthalates are among the estrogen mimics we have created. Because they function to soften plastics, they are added to products such as IV bags, cosmetics, children's pacifiers and toys, and food wraps. Scientists have documented that the sons of mothers exposed to concentrated phthalates have reduced sperm counts and other reproductive abnormalities. Flame retardants, added to children's sleepwear, have also been implicated as reproductive toxins as has Bisphenol A (BPA), a compound in the epoxy resins that are used to line metal food cans, dental sealants, and some water bottles.

The book, *Our Stolen Future,* picks up where *Silent Spring* left off. It documents how we are threatening our health and limiting the future of our children with exposure to these endocrine-disrupting chemicals. But the book was published in 1996, and we still manufacture and use these chemicals. Phthalate-free and BPA-free products have recently become available for consumers who know enough about potential problems to demand a choice in their consumption of them.

Sailing through salt marshes as they slowly slide past, responding to the ceaseless ebb and flow of tide, we see not just single animals or plants of the marsh. Instead, the whole web of connections becomes apparent. I watch ospreys hunt and fish, see them protecting their chicks, observe one feed its mate as she incubates eggs, and I know that the small fish she eats may be loaded with contaminants. For DDT at least, we pulled back from its production once we understood its serious problems, and ospreys have recovered as a result. I see them today because Rachel Carson and others like her worked to alert us to the problems these chemicals cause in ecosystems. I wonder what else ospreys will face as newer chemicals are produced and we use them until we have evidence of their harmful effects. And I wonder what humans will face. Like ospreys, we eat high on the food chain, concentrating chemicals in our food and then our bodies, waiting until we are negatively affected by them to attempt the reduction of their production and use.

In the marshes, life aboard a sailboat is so directly united with the natural world that it is impossible to avoid. All the artifices we have constructed to separate ourselves from nature are stripped away, layer after layer peeled and discarded, until finally reaching the core, the reality. There are no televisions to distract, no other job on which to focus attention, no pile of things that "need to be done." Instead, there are birds wheeling overhead, warm raindrops on an upturned face, multicolored sunsets, a change of wind in the night. These are delights to notice under any conditions, but on a sailboat they are impossible to miss. As we cruise the marshes on the first day of our journey, we sense that powerful bond between ourselves and nature. We are reminded that all humanity is dependent on natural processes, as dependent as are the ospreys, and to be immersed in nature makes it easier to see the connection.

Cruising through the marshes differs from our sailing experiences in Charleston Harbor, where our very first sail on *Velella* was the sea trial, part of the boat-purchasing process. The morning of the sea trial dawned clear and breezy, a perfect chance to test the sails and rigging. Excited, we arrived a bit early at the dock and found Dan, her owner, desperately attempting to install a new bilge pump. We gave him some room, wandering the docks until the broker arrived, then off we sailed into the harbor.

Sailing was relaxing and easy as we moved effortlessly all the way through Charleston Harbor on the starboard tack. A brilliant sun shone brightly over the water in early spring, without the intense heat so common to summer days in the Southeast. Rigging creaked slightly as we shouldered aside small waves formed by the refreshing breeze that filled our sails.

We passed Fort Sumter, where the first shots of the Civil War were fired. When the South officially seceded from the Union, southerners demanded that all U.S. troops be removed, but a group refused to leave the fort. Southern troops fired on the fort, bombarding it for days, until the men inside agreed to evacuate. No one was killed during the bombardment, but Union men were accidentally killed by their own troops during the evacuation. Southerners regarded the repulsion as easy and the conflict nearly bloodless. Unfortunately, both interpretations turned out to be misleading, and our country was thrown into one of the most difficult and bloodiest prolonged wars in our history. If a few individuals can initiate that level of harm, surely a few individuals can also prevent it. Rachel Carson did.

Still reflecting over the role of individuals and the fine line between chaos and calm, we sailed past Fort Moultrie, where Revolutionary War troops held off the better-equipped British fleet. Charleston was founded in 1670 and was a thriving city by 1776. At the beginning of the Revolutionary War, British ships sailed into the important port, but American troops in the fort damaged the English ships and drove the fleet away, in part because the fibrous and spongy palmetto logs from which the fort was built absorbed enemy cannonballs and rendered them harmless. The state flag of South Carolina has a palmetto tree on it to honor the palmetto logs in the fort. The people who now called themselves Americans began to think that they might win their freedom from England, but England was too strong and her ships too many to be defeated easily. It was her sailing ships and command of the seas that made England so strong in the first place. Later in the war, Charleston was blockaded, and American patriots in the city nearly succumbed to despair during its occupation by British troops and their Loyalist supporters.

All that early warfare was conducted between sailing ships and land-based forts, and those ships came close to winning the war for the English. As we dodge shallows in our relatively small sailing boat, secure in the knowledge that if the winds die or shift to a frustrating quarter, we can just crank up the engine, I begin to appreciate how the deep-drafted, engineless British ships were able to maneuver within the harbor and avoid unmarked shoals. As I look toward shore from my own boat, I can imagine the creaking of sails and lines, the shouting of men, the explosions on deck as enemy cannonballs cut holes in sails and splintered wood into thousands of deadly flying fragments. At the same time the ships were receiving blows from shore batteries, their own cannons were being fired back by gunner crews, officers were desperately attempting to keep order above and below decks, a helmsman was steering the ship, and sailors were climbing the rigging to adjust sails. The decks must have been slippery with blood. At what point did they realize that they had to retreat to get beyond the range of the deadly guns onshore?

Reluctantly we turn back at the harbor's mouth, Ed and I envisioning ourselves passing the final sea buoy on some great adventure, but reality returns as we put *Velella* through the wind and come around on the port tack, headed now back through the harbor. We sail smoothly until a powerboat comes tearing toward us on its way out the harbor, and the wake it kicks up rocks us to and fro. We seem to slosh back and forth, rather slowly reacting to the wake.

While the broker, Ed, and I sit peacefully on deck making slight adjustments to the sails to get a little more performance from them, Dan makes a trip below to bring up sodas from the fridge for all of us. Suddenly, he calls up from the companionway that we must change over to the starboard tack. We reply that the course will put us back out to sea but he insists, with a bit of panic in his voice, that we must immediately switch onto the other tack. We oblige, and slowly *Velella* comes through the wind, we settle on the starboard tack, and the broker decides to see if Dan needs help below. When both fail to return, we become suspicious and look below for ourselves. There we see the broker crouching beside the open bilge, frantically pumping the handle to the manual bilge pump while Dan adjusts the hoses to the new bilge pump he had installed. Water laps at the floorboards from the rim of the full bilge.

Thankfully, Dan discovered the fact that we were sinking when he went below to get the drinks and use the head. It never occurred to him that the reason the hose from the original bilge pump looped up high over a hook was to prevent exactly what had just happened. When he installed the new pump, he just dropped the outlet hose straight into the bilge so that the hose made a short, direct run from the pump itself to the thru-hull; after all, why would anyone run the line up a steep incline and double its length? While at dock on an even keel, all the connections were above the waterline, but on the port tack, with the boat heeled over, the outflow for the bilge submerged below the waterline, and without a high loop above water level to break suction, the tubing provided direct *inflow* of seawater siphoning into the bilge. We were plumbed directly to the ocean by way of the thru-hull, a hole in the hull through which bilge water was supposed to be pumped *out*, not flowing in.

While Dan holds a portion of the tubing up out of the bilge to break the inward flow, each of us takes a turn at the manual bilge pump, and we eliminate the water from the bilge. The broker jokes about how close Dan came to losing a sale by sinking the yacht, but Dan doesn't laugh. In fact, he looks a little sick, for there is more yet to do. The sea trial is over, but a haul-out is required for inspection of the bottom. We pull in the sails and crank up the engine.

The boatyard for the haul-out is located on one of the many deep creeks that feed Charleston Harbor. As novices, we are blissfully unaware of the power of the current, especially acting on a boat with *Velella*'s full keel. As we approach the dock, the tide is ebbing strongly. The slip for haul-out angles directly across the current, with an enormous cradle into which we must carefully place the boat. By facing the current, we hold our own and maneuver alongside the dock, but we recognize that turning broadside to the current will give it advantage over the engine.

Dan is nervous, and the broker has little to say. We survey the approach and feel uncomfortable ourselves. We have a narrow slip to enter across the current. We must enter it quickly in order to stay straight and prevent banging up *Velella*'s sides, but can't overshoot it or we will damage the bow. We hope the engine is up to the task, but we really don't know since we've spent the last few hours sailing instead of motoring. Dan encourages Ed to bring *Velella* into the slip rather than handling it himself as the owner, which should have alerted us to potential problems, but because we are already thinking of *Velella* as ours, Ed agrees.

A squat, fire-plug of a man stands on the dock, ready to handle lines and shouting out instructions. I scramble on deck, with Dan's help, placing every rubber fender we have along the downstream side of *Velella*'s hull to cushion us in case we hit the structure. The broker cleats off multiple lines to use in securing the boat to the dock. Ed, as helmsman, stations the broker on stern lines, Dan at midboat to adjust the fenders, and asks me to handle the lines on the bow. It is up to me to throw the first line to the dockmaster.

With all the lines and fenders secure, we take up our positions. Ed throttles the engine full up, turns toward the dock, and the current catches us. Holding a coiled line in one hand, I aim at the dockmaster, lean back, and throw. The line arcs gracefully through the air, but just before reaching the dock, the end tangles and it drops into the water. Oh, no! I scramble to grab a second line. We are rapidly turning out of position even as the bow is entering the slip. Again I throw, and this time the line uncoils perfectly right into the dockmaster's hands.

But by now, the current has us in its grip. The dockmaster leans back, straining at the line, and every muscle in his body pops out like a bodybuilder in competition. His neck muscles and tendons stand out like bones as he grits his teeth and we float, for a moment, perfectly still. Then we start to move forward as, unbelievably, he pulls us in. I pause for a breath until I see that, with the bow turned, the stern is rapidly swinging toward the dock's superstructure, still gripped by the current. The dockmaster also sees the impending crash, cleats off the bow line, then leaps back to grab a stern line from the broker. This time, he throws a coil around a cleat and uses its leverage to help because he has the whole keel against current by now. Again, an incredible effort of unadulterated power pulls our stern against current. I've never seen such a performance of pure muscular strength before or since. My legs tremble weakly from anxiety.

I am standing on deck, recovering from my exertions, when suddenly the dockmaster starts yelling and pointing at me, down at the water, back at me. Confused, I look around the deck, but then I see it too. The first line, now in the water, angles directly back toward the propeller and disappears from view. If the line fouls the prop, it could severely damage it. I start pulling as rapidly as I can, and Ed cuts the motor since we are now safely tied off. Just in time, I lift the tail of the line from the water. Whew! Another close call survived.

Velella passes inspection and even her bottom paint is holding up well, so we float her back in the water within a couple of hours. By then, the slack tide allows us to easily back her out of the slip, turn, and motor back to her home dock. The broker, who also functioned as the inspector, chatters amiably about how the hull is free of blisters and what a sign of quality that is. With the sea trial and the haul-out behind us, we shake hands, finalize the contract, and tie up our new boat.

We experience a few misadventures of our own after buying *Velella*. As a learning method, trials and errors, lots of them, seem to be the most common and effective way to learn. A couple of days after Dan's mistake, we head out again on our own. Now, with some experience under our belts, twenty knots of wind is fine for sailing, but it was way too much for beginners.

We head to the harbor, through a gauntlet of narrow cuts in which the current boils along, pulling us with it, past a busy bridge where only constant vigilance allows us to avoid the other boats who also await its opening, and through a final, twisting stretch packed nearly shore to shore with powerboats and Jet Skis that dart in front of us like housecats leaping across a busy highway. Hitting one seems inevitable. Just reaching the harbor is a challenge, and we have yet to raise the sails! I am a nervous wreck.

Once we have some room and are clear of nearby boats, Ed turns *Velella* into the wind, and I step forward to raise sail. I struggle with raising the heavy mainsail. It seems to take forever, and I must use the winch on the mainmast to do it. After an eternity of seconds and dozens of turns with the winch handle, the big sail is finally up, but flapping noisily and jerking the boom dangerously around the deck. I hurry to get the staysail up, the jib to follow, so that the sails are set and we are under control. In my haste and inexperience, I fail to see that the staysail is fouled around a cleat. When it stalls, I mistakenly assume that it is as heavy as the mainsail, and I put the halyard around the winch, apply the winch handle for a few turns, and promptly rip a hole in the sail when the halyard pulls the sail up while the cleat holds it down. Sweating by now, nervous, I think through my next actions. "I'm so sorry, *Velella*! Okay, so now drop the staysail, get it unfouled and tied off; get the jib up." Mainsail still flapping, wind full in my face, the jib comes up quickly and easily; we fall off the wind and start flying along.

I am frazzled by my sail-handling mishaps, the wind seems bois-terous, the safety of the shoreline distant, and the possibility for er-ror enormous. I need a little time to calm down, but do not recog-nize my own overexcitement. Ed heads below, leaving me alone at the helm as we rip along, suddenly in shoaling water. I frantically call for Ed, then finally realize as the depth-sounder shows seven feet—our draft is about six—that I must tack the big boat by myself. Taking a deep breath, I turn the wheel to move the bow through the wind, release the working jib sheet and tighten up on the other, lazy sheet as the flapping sail comes across to the other side, then straighten out the helm, and off we fly on the new tack. Wow—it works just like it is supposed to! Now this is fun!

Ed rushes back up the companionway to find me with a death's grip on the wheel, knuckles white, jaw clenched, but eyes shining. Only then do I realize that every muscle is strung tight as a bow, and I consciously take a few deep breaths, relinquish the helm, and allow myself to enjoy the ride. Even now, after years of sailing, I still feel a rush of adrenaline in getting sails up and the boat under way. During those few minutes, sails flapping and the deck unsteady under my feet, I feel vulnerable and off-kilter. Once the sails are set and we are under way, *Velella* seems to be in her element, and we in ours.

Charleston is a magnificent old southern city with noteworthy history. It was the first permanent English settlement in South Carolina. The original site of the settlement is preserved as Charles Towne Landing State Park, and a reconstructed sailing ship moored there provides me with a solid example of a historical ship, including its head. Settlers arrived in 1670, selecting a deep creek off the Ashley River to moor their ship and come ashore, later building on the point between the Ashley and Cooper Rivers that is now called The Battery. Charles Towne, however, was not the settlers' first stop. They came in farther north, into shallow Bulls Bay, and settled on what is now Bulls Island. There they built a fort whose remains still exist on the island. They left one hardy soul, Stephen Bull, to chart the area, and the rest of the settlers went farther south, to the Ashley River location that provided better freshwater access and protection from the sea.

Bulls Island is now part of the Cape Romain National Wildlife Refuge. Endangered red wolves were successfully reintroduced, but later removed. The island is accessible only by boat, and when we disembarked to walk around the interior, we stumbled upon incredibly large alligators lounging across most of the roads and paths. We saw a few footprints of wolves, which were still present when we visited, but it was the alligators that held our attention. I've always heard that they can outrun a human over a short distance, and it seems a short distance between us as we edge around them to get to the other side of a freshwater pond they have claimed. Stephen Bull must have been equally impressed, for the alligators of 1670, unmolested by humans, probably surpassed even these monsters in size.

Like ospreys, bald eagles, and brown pelicans, whose populations have all recovered from historic lows, alligator populations have increased as well. Bird populations began to recover in part because DDT was phased out of use in the United States. But birds as well as alligators were also protected from hunting, and this protection from indiscriminate killing made a huge difference, allowing their numbers to increase.

In the winter of 1700–1701, John Lawson arrived in Charleston from England and traveled through the marshes. He stopped at Bulls Island and makes no mention of alligators, but instead of hogs and cows that were pastured there. In just thirty years, settlers had eliminated the alligators, killing them for their skins and meat and to make the island safer for their domestic animals. After a few days in the marshes, Lawson's group paddled their way up the Santee River and eventually left their canoes behind as they traveled overland. Lawson recorded his observations of the plants, animals, landscape, and Native Americans he encountered, producing some of the best documentation of the Carolinas at the time of English colonization.

For example, Lawson records a story about the Sewee tribe, Native Americans who occupied the land north of Charleston to the mouth of the Santee River. Estimated at more than eight hundred prior to contact, a census in 1715 recorded only fifty-seven. Not only were they decimated by European diseases just as were all other tribes of Natives, but they lost a significant portion of their population on a fruitless attempt at trade shortly before Lawson arrived. Observing all the ships coming into Charleston Harbor and frustrated by the unfair deals they were receiving, the Sewee determined that they could make higher profits if, instead of doing business with unscrupulous ship captains, they traded directly with merchants in London. With that goal in mind, they outfitted their canoes with sails, loaded them with supplies and merchandise, and cast off with most of the male population. Just outside the harbor, a squall struck the flotilla, and those men who were not drowned were taken up by a slave ship and sold into slavery in the West Indies.

The Sewee were almost certainly the first people encountered by the Charles Town settlers because they occupied Bulls Bay where the settlers first landed. The Kiawah tribe occupied the land around the Ashley River, where Charles Town was founded. Reports indicate that they welcomed the English because they desired to trade with them, especially for their metal tools and weapons, and hoped that the English could protect them from hostile tribes infiltrating the region. But the Kiawah quickly declined from disease and slavery and were forced to band together with other tribes in the area. This new tribe formed from the remains of others became known by the general name of the Cusabo. This tribe, too, became extinct. The English colonists of Charleston referred to nearby Natives as "Settlement Indians."

Native Americans were the first slaves used around Charleston because their mere presence made them available for exploitation, but their tendency to die from European diseases and to escape into the dense forests made them undesirable for use on the plantations that were developing around Charleston. When the settlers first arrived, they worked with the Westo, an inland tribe known as slave capturers for the Virginia settlement, to procure other Natives in the slave trade, documented with a 1674 agreement. In less than a decade, by 1683, however, the Westo demanded too much from the fledgling colony, making the English inhabitants as uncomfortable about their own safety as the Natives had been for years, and the English allegiance switched to the Savannah tribe. Within another decade, the Savannah followed the Westo and fell from favor. While some of the captured Natives worked the Charleston plantations, far more were shipped to the West Indies to work English plantations there. In the initial years of the colony (1670–1715), more Native Americans were exported from the port of Charleston to the West Indies as slaves than Africans were imported.

The Yamasee (Yemessee) tribe, which lived to the south of Charleston, instigated the Yamasee War in 1715 because of unfair trading practices, slavery, and the murder of Natives. Although they initially lodged legal complaints with English authorities, their plight was ignored, and the Yamasee finally joined with other tribes and launched an attack against the English settlement. But the result of the conflict was that goods, including guns and ammunition, flowing out of Charleston to the Natives stopped. Ironically, the warring Natives depended on the English to resupply them with weapons and bullets, so the war ended with the powerless Natives despairing of their newfound but absolute dependence on the English for necessities. As the numbers of Natives declined dramatically from disease, slavery, and warfare, the depauperate tribes began to unite into new groupings of shared tribal values. One such alliance was the Catawba, a tribe that still exists today.

Within one hundred years of settlement, the plantation lifestyle became well-developed around Charleston, as well as to the north around the newer city of Georgetown. With the Natives decimated, new slaves were needed, and the importation of Africans began in earnest. The first moneymaking crops grown in the area were indigo, which provided a blue dye, and rice. Both demanded heavy labor to grow, and it was African slaves who grew them. West Africans, in particular those from Sierra Leone, were in high demand because they knew how to grow rice. The plantation owners therefore relied not only on the physical labor of their slaves, but also on their knowledge.

Plantation owners to the north of Charleston, however, had a serious problem. They grew crops destined for consumption in major cities and export from their plantations, but had no easy way to get the crops to the shipping port of Charleston. Rivers and inlets to the north of the city were too shallow to allow ships to sail directly ashore. The overland route to Charleston, hauling heavy goods over lengthy, muddy, rutted roads through swampy forests, was slow and inefficient. Some of these plantation owners recognized that a few modifications to the numerous creeks in the region would allow them to move their crops along waterways instead of roadways.

With a captive human work force, plantation owners realized their plans for physically altering the waterways. By the late 1700s, several canals had been cut through the marshes between Georgetown and Charleston. These new canals allowed planters to transport their products to market more easily and opened additional waterways to new fields where rice could be grown, thereby increasing both their profits and the area under cultivation.

These old canals form the basis for the Intracoastal Waterway. It

engineering job apparently had nothing to do with sailing, it is quickly clear that the technical aspects of sailing attracted him to it. He and Joy built their steel boat themselves from scratch as they prepared for retirement, and Tom knows the specifications down to the placement of the last screw. It is a little intimidating, especially since we bought our boat secondhand and are still learning where everything fits and how it works.

When we relate that we are on our first cruise, they reply that they are, too, but theirs is quite a bit more ambitious than ours. Starting out in Galveston, Texas, several months prior, they are currently making their way up the east coast and are paused for a few weeks in Beaufort. They have already completed a long offshore stint in the Gulf of Mexico, rounded the Keys, and made several shorter treks along the east coast. Their objective is to be in New England by late summer and then come back down the coast in November after hurricane season is over. After that, they head into the Caribbean.

But they have a few problems, not the least of which is that Tom really doesn't enjoy sailing. He describes building the boat with pride and pleasure, but each of their sailing stories is dark. Their passage across the Gulf of Mexico was rough and they were seasick throughout, constantly worrying about oil tankers and drilling platforms. They dodged enormous tankers, but once misjudged the size, speed, and heading of a tanker and got closer to it than they felt was prudent. They were never out of sight of platform lights, for thousands of oil platforms are clustered around Galveston and the coast of Louisiana, and they were astounded by the numbers made so visible. On several occasions, they even sailed through miniature oil slicks. The environmental harm caused by our dependence on fossil fuels was impossible for them to ignore and grated on their nerves.

Once they reached the west coast of Florida and escaped the majority of oil platforms, they hoped to come inshore and travel the Gulf ICW, but they ran aground in several locations because their big boat has a draft of eight feet. It got even worse once they reached the Atlantic ICW because the tidal range is greater than in the Gulf;

running aground at low tide was a constant threat. Although the ICW is supposed to be maintained at twelve feet in depth, some sections are half that at low tide. With the ICW mostly ruled out, they now travel offshore from inlet to inlet, and then only to the nearest and deepest marina.

Joy is disappointed that they are unable to traverse the marshes because there is an island she particularly wants to visit. It houses a colony of monkeys. She's heard they are "retired" from a government research program, but it sounds a little fantastic to me. She and Tom have plans to rent a powerboat so that they can visit the island. Maybe Ed and I should go see for ourselves. After all, it is just an afternoon away and we have plenty of time to get south.

When Ed and I return to *Velella* that night, we spread out a chart on the dining table in the main saloon. The way to Monkey Island is well marked and deep, and only about an hour from the marina. "Shall we try it?" Ed asks. "Absolutely!" I reply. "Let's explore the town in the morning, leave here about lunchtime, and anchor there tomorrow night."

"If we anchor on the south side, we'll have time for some sailing in the afternoon, before we anchor. The sound is plenty wide there. What do you think?" Ed asks.

"Let's do it! I wonder what that Monkey Island is like. Do you think we'll really see monkeys?"

Monkey Island

SOMETIMES IN THE SWAMPS OF SOUTH CAROLINA'S LOW-country, time stands still. Ancient live oaks, hirsute with dangling gray locks of Spanish moss, still stand upright after generations of women and men have come and gone and the pull of countless gusts of wind has failed to topple them. Bullbay magnolias stand dark and mute until their huge, bone-white flowers open with a scent that humans and insects alike find irresistible. Dewdrops coalesce from moist night air onto the waxy petals, causing them to shimmer in the moonlight, and this shimmer, combined with the heady scent that grows and expands, is a transport to another realm. In the over-whelming sweetness that oozes from the waxy white petals, the low-country of South Carolina comes alive.

Ghosts linger amid the swamps and forests, phantoms that never quite relinquish their bony grasp on the Old South. A young man racing to his beloved is tragically killed in the surf, but continues to walk windswept beaches to warn of imminent hurricanes; a pale wisp searches the marshes for her lost engagement ring flung away by her angry family, and still rises from her uncomfortable grave: these ghosts are truths to some. Other phantoms, however, are purely anchored in the present even though they are so unexpected that they seem illusory. They blur the distinction of dream and reality. Such phantoms as these we have come to know in our sailing adventures through the salt marshes of the Southeast.

In the lowest reaches of the lowcountry, vast rivers empty into huge and desolate sounds. The river water is black as ink, changed forever by its prolonged stay in the endless swamps and marshes. Light can only penetrate a few inches beyond the surface of these black rivers. Nothing is visible in the inky water, but swirls and disturbances of its surface indicate that animals, both small and large, are hungrily feeding on each other. Life and death are inseparable here, as everywhere.

In one of the largest and most isolated of the South Carolina sounds, Saint Helena Sound, an island rises out of the expanse of marsh and river. Spreading live oaks trail their mossy branches into the dark water, and tall pines, straight as puritanical backbones, are juxtaposed with the stocky, slouching palmettos that are scattered across the island's back. Most of its shoreline is shrouded by spartina, but where there are breaks in the marsh grass, expanses of sand extend down to the water's edge. Stacks of driftwood and mounds of shell are piled along the steep southeastern edge of the island by the strong currents that sweep along the shore. The eastern tip merges into an extensive flat of spartina and then into a huge mudflat visible only at low tide. This spit reaches out into the endless, empty sound, stretches toward the open sea, and divides the sound into two wide rivers, both of which flank the island. Most of the island is marsh, but about 350 acres qualify as true land.

In a sailboat easing silently in on the last whispers of a breeze, the quiet splash of an anchor is all that disturbs the ominous quiet of the gathering dusk. In the distance, on the mainland, cicadas are calling with their rhythmic, rasping buzz, but here a deathlike silence is complete. Rows of buoys that mark crab pots are indicators of the transition from deep to shallow water, where blue crabs abound. The deep water runs close alongside the island's southern shore, and the boat rides to her anchor just beyond the first row of pots, little more than a stone's throw away from the island's edge.

An unearthly, prehistoric squawk erupts from directly overhead, and without a thought I crouch down low to the deck while glancing back over my shoulder. With an immense span of wings, serpentine neck, and dangling legs, an approaching great blue heron seems more like a pterodactyl than a feathered bird. Those otherworldly, harsh calls sporadically uttered in the dead of night are loud and eerie enough to wake a light sleeper and will haunt the dreams of those thus awakened. Simultaneously with the arrival of the great blues, black-crowned night herons emerge from their daytime roosts to begin their nightly search for prey. Perched along the shore, their necks folded tightly against their bodies, they look at a distance like hunched-up, withered old men, able to cast a spell or evil eye on whomever they choose.

Great vultures fill the air overhead as they glide noiselessly into their night resting place. Like all daytime birds, these too cease their routine activity as the sun departs, but their sudden, silent appearance is disconcerting nevertheless. They create an uneasy premonition, a slight, nagging suggestion that may linger into the realm of sleep and be transformed in dreams. Turkey vultures soar on stationary, outstretched wings held in the perfect "V" of a child's drawing, spiraling down slowly before vanishing into the dark center of the island, like matter drawn into the invisibility of a black hole. Black vultures, a second species, are also caught in the dusky whirlpool, but seem to resist their descent by frequently flapping their short, broad wings that are highlighted at the tips.

Although the vultures are eventually swallowed by the island cauldron, our imaginations conjure up the turkey vultures' hooked beaks, big black bodies, and the wrinkled, hemorrhagic skin of their naked red heads. Equally disturbing, the bare skin on the heads of black vultures is black and wrinkled, like the head of an unwrapped mummy. The nakedness of the birds' heads enables them to reach deep inside carcasses without fouling their feathers with blood and gore.

Flocks of noisy boat-tailed grackles, as if caught in a countercurrent, rise up from the island and fly to the mainland on their evening commute. The small birds do not sleep the night on the island. When the last flight of the day has departed, a sole straggler suddenly hops up from the island and, with a succession of panicked chirps, hurriedly flies after his departing companions. He flies after them urgently, as if afraid to be left behind, alone, on the island.

With the departure of the last flock of grackles, the sun is swallowed by the dark river. The clear sky with its wispy clouds betokens a fair evening, but the island itself seems sinister and foul. Vultures are there, waiting for the morrow, and the only sounds are "uncouth, explosive cries of heron in the night silence," as described by Richard Perry in *At the Turn of the Tide*, which seem to come less from a living bird than from a shadowy spirit of the marsh. As night falls, the individual trees blur together as the island morphs into a uniform, dark mass.

In the shimmering moonlight, the island exhales silently, and its breath condenses into a low fog, whose tendrils wrap around the island and snake into its interior. The fog emerges from the lungs of the marsh, the grass itself, with the thickest fog woven between blades of spartina. Some wisps stream across the surface of the calm river, turning the whole scene into an image of a barely steaming witch's brew. The weird sisters' charm is wound up tight to make a fair evening into a foul night.

Suddenly, the island bursts into a cacophony of sound. Screeches and screams of terror, blood-curdling howls of rage, and crashes of falling branches come from deep within the island. The noise increases in volume as the sounds shift from the island's center toward its edge, and the anchorage. The unearthly cries, the strange groans, and the movement of countless bodies through the underbrush sound in close proximity to the island's shore. Has the forest come alive, transformed into a charging troop of men wielding daggers, swords, and pikes as Macbeth experienced? Just as the frightening sounds reach a crescendo, they abruptly stop, as if daggers had pierced the bodies and drained away the lifeblood of the terror-stricken horde. Throughout the night, the episodes of terror and calm are repeated, but their frequency is greatest during the early evening and just before dawn: they are crepuscular.

As the long-awaited dawn arrives, culprits of the night's disturbance become visible along the water's edge. With smoke-rings of fog still wreathing the island, ghostly faces appear among tree branches in the mist. These small faces, so reminiscent of human form through distant, haunting memory, seem startlingly out of place. It is like looking into the past and seeing distortions of ourselves. Surely they are ghosts and this is only a dream.

While the morning sun warms the island and disperses lingering fog, a troop of rhesus-macaque monkeys moves out of the forest to join the group on the beach that is foraging peacefully along the river. I can hardly believe that they are real. Relief floods through me as the melee of last night suddenly make sense. My bizarre dreams are just that—dreams.

A mother with a tiny, pink-faced baby clinging to her belly walks along on all fours, stopping frequently to adjust the newborn infant. She is approached by several others who are allowed to observe, but not to touch the infant. One monkey in particular is fascinated and frequently tries to touch the small form. When the mother bares her teeth and threatens the intruder, it moves a few feet away where it can still observe the infant, but, strangely, it shreds a leaf with its fingers and teeth as it continues to watch the pair. Is it a threat to them? Would it have harmed the baby if the mother had allowed it to touch the infant?

Several young, half-grown monkeys chase each other up spindly trees, leaping from limb to limb in a breathtaking show of acrobatics. One finally pounces from an overhanging limb onto an unsuspecting comrade who is resting at the base of the tree turned jungle gym. This one turns on his attacker, and together they go flying up the nearest tree trunk, chattering excitedly, while the now-pursued aggressor seems to delight in the havoc he caused. They must be equivalent to teenage humans.

A big, silvery-haired male patrols the beachfront, occasionally barking and growling at other monkeys. He charges a fellow half his size who is sitting silently in a sunny spot suddenly desired by the silver male. The challenged monkey darts off without so much as a grumble while the attacker barks after him. When he plops down to claim the seat he won, a slim female lacking the hairy ruff of the male approaches and grooms him. With the exception of the grumpy male, his grooming partner, and the jabbering young acrobats, the rest of the troop quietly and efficiently searches for tasty items that might make breakfast.

Dozens of monkeys are perched in the treetops, searching for succulent new leaves. One discovers a slow-moving moth, and calmly plucks off four huge wings and drops them from its perch before popping the remaining insect body into its mouth. While the monkey chews on the morsel, it leans over to watch the big wings spiral slowly toward the ground.

Every treetop has a monkey in it. Some are seated on branches so slender that they bend under the monkey's slight weight. Occasionally a monkey leaps into another tree across a gap that makes me gasp. They are easily sixty feet above the ground. One youngster misses the limb he was aiming for, leaves tearing from his grasp as he falls, but just a few feet lower, another branch offers a handhold, and his descent is interrupted. He calmly seats himself on that limb as if the fall was neither unexpected nor terrifying. He does not worry about the past or the future, secure only in the moment. I envy him.

The morning sun stirs up a gentle breeze, and *Velella* tugs against her anchor rode as her bow swings toward the island, as if she wants a better look herself. The young acrobats suddenly cease their frantic chases and move carefully to the water's edge to investigate. They peer intently toward the boat, adjusting their bodies and cocking their heads to assure themselves of the best angle of view. Smiling at our similarities, I peer back at them through binoculars, shifting position whenever the object of my attention becomes obstructed from view.

One very brave fellow climbs out to the tip of a tree branch that overhangs the water. When the strange river creatures do not respond, he begins to shake the branch, leaning out toward the boat, daring us to react. We move, and he shrieks, then scurries back down the tree and peeks out from behind the base of its trunk. Overcome by curiosity, he once again moves back up into the tree, becoming bolder as we sit quietly. Soon he is again shaking branches at us. This excites the attention of several other youngsters, who also rush to command posts in the dead tree branches. Together they howl, chatter, and shake branches until they tire of the game and our nonresponsiveness and return to their foraging in the grass.

This is a breeding colony of rhesus-macaque monkeys, introduced onto the island in 1979 to provide animals for biomedical research (slightly different from Joy's description of "retired" monkeys). It is the only breeding colony of free-ranging rhesus monkeys in the United States. The monkeys were originally imported by a private company specializing in breeding primates for use in research. The monkeys are now owned by the U.S. Food and Drug Administration, but the private company contracts to maintain the colony.

Rhesus-macaque monkeys normally live in India and are hardy enough to withstand the occasional cold spells of lowcountry winters. Although they can swim, it is a long way to another island, which I suppose must keep the monkeys contained. The island is isolated by large rivers within the open sound; they'd have to cross a huge expanse of water, and I doubt that any would make the attempt. Should they escape, however, there is nothing to prevent their colonization of other islands.

This large colony of about 3,200 animals, composed of several troops, is supported by food delivered daily to the island by boat. The monkeys scour the forest clean of anything edible, which may account for the silence of insects here. The grackles, however, have learned that monkey chow is easily convertible to grackle chow, as long as they move faster than the monkeys. The mosquitoes, too, must be delighted by all that warm, bitable monkey flesh. A study published in 2008 found that levels of fecal coliform bacteria were higher in the creeks surrounding the island than in the larger rivers themselves, but never exceeded a level considered harmful. The canopy cover of large trees had actually increased, but the understory vegetation, which we saw more affected by the colony, was not evaluated.

The monkeys spend an hour or more searching for food in the treetops, then descend to the forest floor, where they sit quietly in the sunshine. One particularly old and feeble fellow stretches out in the sun, his legs and arms extended, as if the warming sun relieves his aching joints—so much toil and trouble even to move. Juveniles spend the majority of their time climbing trees, jumping from limbs, dangling from branches, and leaping on one another. Older monkeys groom each other, feed, or just rest.

Suddenly, the peaceful scene becomes chaotic as monkeys leap into trees, screeching wildly, and rush back into the forest, tree limbs cracking and bowing from their passage. A rival troop emerges on the beach and rushes briefly after the fleeing first troop. A big hairy male leads the charge, but smaller monkeys participate in the threats as well. After a few minutes of intimidating calls and shaking of tree limbs, the source of the night's noise, the second group settles down to feed. As the sun rises and the air heats up, this troop, too, moves slowly back into the forest.

During the afternoon, monkeys sporadically appear on the beach to search for anything left stranded by the retreating tide. Occasional battles between troops, the outcome seemingly determined by the most noise a troop can make, occur across the island throughout the day. Glimpses of monkeys fleeing with other monkeys pursuing, and sudden flocks of startled grackles shrieking in the treetops, indicate where different troops have moved in the island's interior. In general, however, the monkeys are not nearly as visible as in the early morning.

During the late afternoon's low tide, monkeys again appear on the beach, which is widened by the water's retreat. They move deep into the now-dry spartina, each individual's path marked by gently swaying blades. An occasional brown head pokes up above green grass, and often a tiny hand reaches up to pluck a morsel from a tip that has been bent down toward the feeding monkey. A few of the largest animals come right down to the river's edge, where the mark of low water delineates the spartina's growth zone. There they turn over oyster shells and inspect a few dead stems of grass that are caught between the water and living blades. Only a thin strip of mud separates the river from marsh grass where the monkeys feed, but the animals do not transgress this boundary. They stay clear of the mud and water, preferring to remain either within the marsh grass or on the island itself.

As night comes again, the monkeys grow quiet, the birds make their commutes, and silence reigns. With the fall of darkness, however, the island again erupts with frightening noise. Falling asleep is difficult. I wake abruptly to the thought of small, hairy hands reaching up from the black, ghostly river to grasp the anchor chain. Am I awake?

Beaufort and Environs

"I hate to ask this, but I just can't figure this one out. I've never seen anyone take a shovel onto a boat before! What are you planning to do?" The preeminent head of the marina yard crew, an astute and curious observer, follows me down the long dock as I push a rickety cart full to overflowing with unusual equipment. Along with the shovel balanced precariously on top, a big square sieve made of wood and metal screening occupies one entire side of the cart and hangs out over the forward edge. Two sturdy microscopes and an assortment of buckets and bags complete the assemblage. The wheels of the cart bow outward like the legs on an old nag sent to pasture, and the handle is loose where screws are tearing out of rotten wood, but ever-present duct tape holds the thing together. It bumps along as the wheels hit each wooden slat in the dock.

With each bump, the gear settles deeper into the belly of the cart, threatening to push the sides even farther apart, and the shovel's position is more precarious as its balance shifts. Descending the last steep incline, I lean backward to counterbalance the heavy weight of the gear, and the shovel begins to slide. Instinctively, I quit fighting gravity, lean forward, and run with the cart to the bottom of the inclined dock, landing safely on the flat surface of the floating dock where the boats are tied. The shovel wobbles, then settles in between the sieve and the cart's side, secure at last, and I reply, "I know this gear is unusual on a boat, but we are going out to collect animals for our students back at the university."

"You mean fish?"

"No, mostly clams, snails, crabs, and worms. We dig them up from the mudflats, which is why we need the shovel and the rest."

The dockhand retains his rather quizzical look as he helps us cast off, and we motor away, too encumbered by gear on the deck to sail. We are heading out to collect marine invertebrate animals to use in both research and teaching.

Expanses of mud and sand exposed by a retreating tide call to us like sirens: "Beach your boat and come ashore this misty isle!" Helpless against them, we pore over charts of inlets and bays, searching for a dotted line, surrounding green, which indicates a shoal. The area around Beaufort is full of easily accessible but well-marked shoals, and several inlets provide access to clean seawater that sweeps regularly across the flats to deliver oxygen and nutrients. It was this proliferation of rich mudflats that attracted us to Beaufort and held us there, making it our home port.

The mudflats are teeming with animals, but most of them are revealed only by shovel and sieve and only at low tide, which is why we carry the strange implements. As the tide falls lower, we eagerly approach a nearby mudflat and wait until the muddy floor of the salt-marsh estuary emerges above the water's reach, when we can walk about for an hour or so. This murky realm that most humans rarely contact, except, perhaps, with their boat hulls, and then with displeasure rather than the keen anticipation we experience, is a realm of diverse and fantastic animals. We fell in love with the area precisely because of the muddy flats and sandy shoals—the bane of most other boaters!

In addition to its alluring mudflats, Beaufort also attracted us with its charming waterfront. In one interesting establishment, I consider an enormous shark tooth of *Megalodon* estimated at about 25 million years old, along with a plate carved from a solid conglomeration of coiled ammonites and a polished slab of straight-shelled *Orthoceras,* both relatives of the chambered nautilus about 400 million years old. Then I discover a hardbound copy of Sir Alister Hardy's classic *The Open Sea: Its Natural History,* published in 1965. The book contains wonderful watercolor plates that beautifully illustrate thorough descriptions of the ocean's natural history.

There I discover that the animal *Velella* presented a quandary for biologists because some thought it was a colony of genetically related but distinct individuals while others believed it to be a single individual that had developed multiple mouths and other organs. Not until Hardy's time was it shown conclusively to be a single individual who just appeared to be a colony. All its separate mouths and tentacles, all those components that seem to be distinct, are, in reality, one.

It is a good metaphor for how we feel. Ed and I began by sharing a dream, an ill-defined, but definite sense that sailing is an avenue to discovery. Although we start out as two individuals and a boat, we soon suspect that we are not as distinct as we first thought. While we may look like two people aboard a boat, we are, in reality, a single sailing unit, all of us working together to accomplish our goals. As in any good relationship, we downplay our egos for the benefit of the greater whole. This is a hard task, to stop asserting what *I* want and to think instead of what *we* need. The only way to ensure both a safe and enjoyable sail, however, is to do just that—to recognize the symbiosis and willingly become part of a larger whole.

For naturalists, it might be expected that this glimmering of insight spurs us to examine who we are in relation to the natural world. In addition to our technical books on sailing and piloting, as well as several coastal field guides, we also have aboard books that include essays and poetry by writers such as Emerson, Thoreau, Whitman, Wordsworth, and Coleridge as well as other books pertaining to Western and Eastern thought. These books are our companions as we strive to relate our experiences in nature to our views on nature.

Learning to sail is a way of learning to see. I look at the set sails and see how the wind fills them. I watch the tell-tales, bits of string attached to the sails that flutter evenly when the sails are properly set, and see the air flowing over them. I look at the clouds overhead and see their shapes and colors and direction they move. I look at the water and see the frothy bubbles flowing past, and dolphins riding our bow wave, and jellies floating by serenely.

It is the going that is important, not just the arrival point and time. A slower pace, in fact, allows more time to see. By slowing down, by appreciating each moment, by considering before acting, by thinking of others, we have the beginnings of a philosophy. We have much to learn, but are under way, with *Velella* as our teacher.

Perhaps it was that first perfect day of our cruise, when we left Charleston and arrived at Beaufort, that colored our glasses rosy, or the discovery of an ammonite plate and a favorite book in the same waterfront shop. Maybe it was the strange, mysterious evening we spent anchored by Monkey Island. Almost certainly it was the proliferation of animals on the many mudflats. For all those reasons and more, we decide to move to Beaufort, South Carolina, as our home port and make arrangements with a marina there. "Beau" as in beautiful, and not to be confused with Beaufort, North Carolina. There "Beau" is pronounced as in "Beauregard" or as in "a girl's beau."

Beaufort's founders selected a bend of the Beaufort River for the site of their town. Deep water runs close along the outside curve and tosses up a bluff on which the oldest homes are safely perched. On the shallow, inner curve of the river, a sandy shoal almost directly across from the waterfront is a popular spot to beach shallow-draft powerboats. Whether in the downtown marina or the anchorage tucked alongside, we hear laughter and music drifting across the water from the shoal as revelers splash in the shallows.

Each year, Beaufort accentuates the summer season with a water festival. Posters advertising the water festival abound in the marina office. The highlight of the festival, which concludes on the last weekend of July, is the Boat Parade and Blessing of the Fleet.

Outrageously decorated, barely floating hulks intermingle with expensive yachts in a short, watery parade route around the harbor. Nearly every resident we meet in our new marina has a story to tell about a previous Boat Parade, and all of them encourage us to return from our summer cruise by then.

Beaufort, like Charleston, is an old city of old money; it was the second town chartered in South Carolina after Charleston. We spend our first full day in the town on a walking tour of the waterfront and historical homes. Magnificent antebellum houses, with sweeping entrances, gaze out over the water. One has an official plaque that reveals it was the setting for the movie *The Big Chill*. Enormous live oak trees, several hundred years old, sag beneath their age and weight, propped up with limbs that reach the ground. The shade they provide robs the sun of its intensity, cooling the homes beneath them, and we pause gratefully to sip from our water bottles while admiring the view. Blocks of tabby support the houses and the huge columns that bear the weight of the roof.

Tabby is composed of oyster shells mortared together by sand, water, and lime. Beaufort was the center of tabby construction, for British settlers found no stones for constructing their buildings. They did, however, find piles of oyster shells left by Native Americans and used the discarded shells as the basis for tabby. Like the big live oaks, the sprawling old mansions require some extra support in the languid heat, and tabby provides it. Similarly, Spanish settlers in St. Augustine also built with tabby (in addition to coquina rock), and it is their word "tapia," which means "mud wall," from which our English word is derived.

Before we depart from our new marina to resume our cruise, we receive a day of rain that is heavy enough to make sailing difficult. Ed decides to tackle an engine job that will improve its efficiency, and I leave to give him some room. The rain is pounding so hard in the slowly draining marina parking lot that when I step off the sidewalk, I am ankle-deep in water. The whole town seems to be sinking into the river. I catch myself humming, "If it keeps on raining, I think the whole damn [town] is gonna float away," a modification of a line from a favorite song by Iris DeMent. I go no farther than the marina's lounge, snuggle into a comfortable chair, and decide that such a profoundly rainy day is my chance to study Beaufort's human history.

The lowcountry of South Carolina is so named because it is low and wet, cut through by creeks and marshes. Most of the land is barely above the mark of high tide, which sweeps across the marshes and piles up into the creeks. Beaufort is just one of several old towns that rest on high ground of an island. Today, roads and bridges connect them, but the Sea Islands along the South Carolina and Georgia coasts and into northern Florida were historically rather isolated. They communicated with each other and the outside world through the ships that came into their ports.

Just south along the ICW from Beaufort, still easily accessible by water, is Port Royal, one of the oldest European settlements still in existence. Its port occasionally receives ships, but not nearly as many it did during the height of cotton export. Instead, today it is a fishing village, its docks filled with shrimp boats and trawlers. Another boater in the lounge tells me that the old dock supports a great seafood restaurant, which only adds to my interest in visiting the town either by boat or by car.

In Port Royal's heyday as a bustling port, it exported Sea Island cotton, which was grown on surrounding islands. By 1786, the height of Sea Island cotton growth, indigo had fallen out of favor because it was no longer exported to England as a result of our war with them. Rice followed suit, for it, too, was exported. Cotton, however, was not solely an export, but also part of local and regional trade in the manufacture of cloth. Thus Port Royal, as the center of Sea Island cotton export, continued to grow in importance. But soon another type of cotton was developed that did not require the long, hot growing climate that restricted Sea Island cotton to coastal islands. Green or upland cotton, as it was called, could be grown far inland and was planted across the state. It was the forerunner of modern cotton grown today. With the advent of easier-to-grow upland cotton and the development of the cotton gin to extract seeds from its shorter cotton fibers, demand for Sea Island cotton plummeted and Port Royal declined in importance.

At approximately the same time that the southern economy was shifting inland, away from the coast, the Civil War (1861–65) freed the slaves who worked plantations. As the economies of coastal towns ground to a halt, wealthy Confederates with the ability to move abandoned Port Royal for greener pastures. Freed slaves, who had been viewed all along as economic machinery rather than people, were abandoned just as readily. They were left behind with no opportunities to earn a wage and no way to escape from crushing poverty accentuated by war.

Practically the only way to survive was small-scale farming, but as wealthy northern industrialists swept south during the era of Reconstruction, they also ignored the plight of poor blacks and whites who were farming the abandoned plantation land although they did not own it. The new landowners exploited the farmers as sharecropping became common. The sharecroppers paid their "rent" for use of land by turning over most of their crops to an often-absentee landowner who squeezed profit out of the subjugated people. They could never earn enough to free themselves from the system, perpetuating yet another form of slavery.

In 1862, the Pennsylvania Freedmen's Relief Association built a school for freed slaves in the Port Royal area to alleviate some of the staggering inequality in education and wealth. Its objective was to provide education to former slaves, allowing them to earn a living and buy the land that they had worked for so many years. Unfortunately, but perhaps not surprisingly, no person educated by the Penn School was able to buy land because the slavery-sharecropping system was too deeply embedded in the economy. Realizing that education was of utmost importance in building toward economic equality, the Penn School continued to focus on training people in industrial and agricultural education until 1948, when it became the Penn Community Services Center. In the 1960s, it hosted a variety of civil rights retreats for such notable figures as Dr. Martin Luther King Jr., Jesse Jackson, and others, and it was recognized as a National Historic Landmark in 1974. The Penn Center still exists today, and its current mission is to promote and preserve the history and culture of the Sea Islands, particularly the Gullah culture. They celebrated a sesquicentennial in 2012.

I pause from my historical study when the door to the marina lounge flies open, accompanied by wind, rain, and an overweight, red-faced guy in a yellow slicker. He looks like a lemon with legs. He stomps his feet, shakes water off his slicker, curses the weather, and complains bitterly about how no one was on the dock to handle lines for him so that he scratched the hull of his expensive yacht while docking. He can't dock his own boat? Then he proceeds to explain that his wife won't set foot in the marina bathrooms because "common" people use them. He is an embarrassing reminder that wealth and boating often go hand in hand and that some confuse prosperity with worth. I shrink down behind my pile of books and laptop computer so that I have a reason to avoid speaking to him. He heads back out in a huff when he can elicit no response from me.

Although Beaufort was chartered in 1711, Port Royal claims 1562 as its date of founding. In that year, a group of French Huguenots built a fort called Charlesfort, but abandoned it within a year and attempted to return to France. In 1566, Spaniards seized the abandoned fort and built their town of Santa Elena, where they survived for more than twenty years. Remains of this settlement have been unearthed on Parris Island, which is now an active archaeological site that the public can visit. Santa Elena flourished until 1587, when the Spanish settlers were recalled to St. Augustine, Florida, to retrench their forces after Sir Francis Drake's damaging raids for the English, who were themselves attempting to establish a colony farther north in the Carolinas. The English tried three times, from 1585 to 1590, to settle a colony on Roanoke Island in North Carolina. Each failed, the last with the disappearance of the Lost Colonists. Once the English defeated the Spanish Armada in 1588, they felt a little more secure in their ability to rout the Spanish in the New World, and it was 1607 before they tried and succeeded in establishing the first permanent English colony at Jamestown, Virginia. Port Royal was settled yet again, this time by Scots, in 1682 as Stuart Town. The Spanish attacked and eliminated Stuart Town four years later in 1686 by burning it to the ground, but the English rebuilt it. The old Spanish town name of Santa Elena persists today as two namesakes, a sea island called St. Helena, and St. Helena Sound, both just north of Beaufort.

While the French, English, and Spanish fought over the region, the people who already lived there lost ground to warfare, slavery, settlements, and, most significantly, disease. Since these coastal tribes were among the first to interact with Europeans, their numbers were reduced almost immediately following contact. Thomas Harriot, in his narrative of the first Roanoke Island expedition in 1585, records that when the English left a Native town, as much as half the population sickened and died. He was writing about the Carolina Algonquin tribes along the North Carolina coast, but the Natives that lived around St. Augustine and Santa Elena experienced the same conditions. Between Charleston and Beaufort there was a diversity of tribes, which included the Sewee, Wando, Etiwan, Kiawah, Edisto, Stono, Ashepoo, Combahee, Wimbee, Escamacu (St. Helena Indians), and Yamasee. All of these tribes became extinct shortly after Charleston and Beaufort were settled, except for the Yamasee. They persisted until the Yamasee War of 1715, when that tribe lost its war against the English and dispersed, any survivors moving inland to join other tribes.

I am interested to learn about the human history, but it is the natural history of marine animals that draws us here, and I long to get back out onto the water and the mudflats. By the end of the day, the rain eases, I return to *Velella*, and over dinner that night at the restaurant in Port Royal, we plan a mudflat excursion to collect animals.

Ed and I teach biodiversity and invertebrate zoology by introducing our students to the other strange inhabitants with whom we share the planet. We collect animals, show them to our students, and then return the animals to the same place from which we removed them. The living animals are so much more interesting and provide more opportunities to engage students than does a laboratory jar of pickled worms.

Those sandy, muddy shoals around Beaufort are home to untold numbers of many different types of animals. They live buried in the sediment, living out their lives mostly unnoticed and ignored, unconcerned by our ignorance. They are as different from each other as sponges and worms, anemones and snails, clams and fish. As large land animals, we tend to think of birds and mammals as "different," but in the sea, a true and mind-boggling diversity exists. Both birds and mammals, after all, have the same number of limbs, comparable body coverings, and similar internal organs and processes. A segmented worm may have hundreds of legs while a clam has none, a snail has a hard shell while the delicate tentacles of a jelly are both easily damaged yet full of stinging cells, and a fish has an internal skeleton of bone while an anemone's skeleton is made of water.

As naturalists, we revel in biodiversity and, as professors, we strive to teach others to appreciate and conserve it. There is joy in the initial discovery of natural variety. We have held the living lampshell, *Glottidia*, who has survived virtually unchanged for 500 million years, picked up awning clams that look like amber fingernails, watched tube anemones emerge from their muddy homes like animated blooming chrysanthemums, dug up six-foot-long acorn worms that reek of iodine and breathe with gill slits like fish, and placed countless sizes and kinds of bristle worms, some with stunning opalescence, others with fishlike scales, in tanks for our students to study. Add to these the snap and pop of pistol shrimp discharging their cocked claws at a perceived intruder or the thumbnail-sized young of horseshoe crabs bulldozing soft mud like reincarnated trilobites. These are but a few of the wonders of a mudflat that we take back to show our students.

Seeing and hearing that diversity is like learning to hear and enjoy great music. For enthusiasts, the rewards are much the same. At first, the sheer diversity is overwhelming and all-encompassing, much like the virtuoso performance of an outstanding composer or performer, but then, after becoming familiar with diversity, interactions between individuals, their environment, and other species move to the forefront like the recognition of harmony and intricacy of form. The knowledge of the community as a whole—ecological knowledge—is subtle but no less sublime than the beauty presented directly to the senses.

For ourselves as well as our students, the rewards of study are born from willingness to take the time to look. Every exposure to biodiversity builds like a wave that feels the touch of the beach. Just as molecules of water pile higher and higher upon each other until the wave breaks forward and spills onto the beach, so each observation adds together until synthesis and understanding spill forth.

Imagine a classroom full of aquaria. Sea stars climb the glass sides and extend an arm, with an eye on its tip, out into the dry air before exploring the other side of the tank. Sea urchins graze like porcupines on pieces of lettuce. Jellies swim in tall tanks and accept small bits of shrimp from nervous fingertips. The heart of a bristle worm pulses steadily under a microscope, moving red blood throughout its transparent body. Suddenly, the room is full of questions and observations. A blond boy in a baseball cap is urgently tugging at my shoulder to "Come see this!" A quiet girl has spent a half hour on a single elaborate drawing of a brilliantly colored worm crawling through a forest of algae. She asks what it is called.

The surprisingly colorful bristle worms spend their lives immersed in the dark mud of the estuary, and become visible to us only after they are unearthed like gems by our shovels. Some live in ice-cream cones made of sand grains and close the mouth of their cone-shaped homes with golden bristles. Others look like miniature pieces of bamboo, long segments marked with distinct bands where they touch each other. There are worms that live in cellophane-like tubes, their incredible bodies shaped to fit so that their movements

A Mudflat in Beaufort

THE SUN IS WARM ON MY TANNED SKIN, AND THE GENTLY breaking waves impart a slow rhythm in my brain. I breathe in as each wave moves up the beach, back out as each wave slips back to the sea. Slow, constant breathing, inhaling deeply and noticing the slight sea tang in the air, transports me.

I peer into the sand in front of me. Staring at it, individual grains, pink, orange, purple, gray, or white, emerge from the uniform background. In my mind, they grow in size until they appear as large as boulders, which rest against each other unevenly to create a labyrinth with cavernous spaces. Slipping around one of the boulders, I emerge in such a cavern to be confronted by a bear! This bear looks a little strange, however, with eight legs instead of four, and with gigantic claws adorning all those legs. Instead of a mouth full of teeth, the mouth of this bear has a long sword with which it can impale its prey. It is a tardigrade, or water bear. I duck quickly behind another boulder, and there find a protozoan, made of only one long, skinny cell with a head-like bulge on one end, but just as big as all the other, multicellular animals that abound here.

Almost every group of animals, from anemones to shrimplike copepods, is represented in this Lilliputian world, and exquisite creatures with outlandish names like gastrotrichs and kinorhynchs are found nowhere else but here. The citizens of this world are either long and slender or very flat so that they can slip through the narrow spaces between the grains of sand. Most even have sticky toes so that they can adhere to a sand grain if a wave washes over and disturbs their world. These microscopic denizens of the beaches are called interstitial animals because they live within the interstices, or spaces, between the sand grains. They do not push the sand grains aside while moving about, as bigger animals do when they dig burrows. Instead, they crawl and slip through the channels of the labyrinth, whose architecture changes with each crashing wave. They are creatures so small that a microscope is needed to see them, but most sandy swimming beaches are swarming with them. Underneath an average beach towel, the sand is alive with several million interstitial animals.

Bigger animals live in the beach sand, too. Not only are these animals visible to the naked eye, but so are the trails they leave behind as they displace the sand while digging. A groove carved into the sand ends at a small lump, and I stick my finger in it and pull out an Atlantic auger snail. The pale-gray, cone-shaped, twisted shell narrows down to a sharp point, resembling an archaic auger or drill bit, but one that crawls away. A wider furrow intrigues me and I follow it to its end, where I dislodge a firm white mass of slimy tissue. As I hold the rather unappetizing piece of what could be pork fatback that has acquired mobility, it contracts a little to reveal a tiny portion of the beautiful white shell of a baby's ear, one of the most delicate and attractive of snail shells when empty of its living occupant.

Such creatures thrive on many beaches, but the best beaches are those with the seemingly impossible combination of remoteness and proximity. The beach should be remote from the pressures imposed by shell collectors and sun bathers, but close to the ocean, and the best beaches are usually near the mouth of an inlet. Protected from the direct, pounding ocean waves, but flushed by pure ocean water with each tidal cycle, such a beach has all the advantages of contact with the great ocean and few of the disadvantages. Pure seawater floods the beach sand on the incoming tide, bringing oxygen and the right concentration of salt for marine bodies, while estuarine water flows over it on the outgoing tide, delivering nutrients from the land. It is composed of the perfect combination of coarse-grained sand, which allows the passage of water and oxygen through the sediment, and fine-grained mud, full of organic material on which the animals feed. Unlike the beaches that front the ocean directly, however, it is only rarely disturbed by heavy waves.

We have discovered such a fabulous flat near Beaufort, which includes a great anchorage for *Velella*. Our perusal of charts indicates that we can anchor her in fifteen feet of water just a hundred yards from the sandflat. Like a mother with a small child, I am most comfortable when I can keep an eye on her, close enough to help should I be needed. I worry too much about an imagined scenario—*Velella* drifting out to sea, leaving us stranded on the sandflat as the water starts to rise.

Our first attempt to access the fabulous flat nearly results in disaster. Rounding the last protected bend in the river, the sound gapes open ahead of us as a strong wind blows in from offshore. Waves roll us side to side and a crash comes from below as the stove rocks hard on its gimbals. Under normal conditions, the gimbals allow the stove to adjust to the angle at which the boat is heeled over, but the short, choppy waves knock it back and forth too harshly. Spray from a particularly rough wave sweeps across my face but dries quickly on the stiffening wind. Refusing to believe our senses, we fight our way out to the site, determined to go ashore.

Once we nose into about fifteen feet of water, I go forward to set the anchor. The tide is still racing out, but the wind is pushing in the opposite direction. I drop the hook and pay out the rode, but the current pushes us up over the anchor in the wrong direction. Typically, we let the anchor rode pay out while the boat drifts behind it, then Ed puts her in reverse to set the anchor in the bottom. This time, we can't back down on the anchor because we are up over the top of it, and the anchor rode might foul around the prop. I have no idea whether the anchor is set or dragging on the bottom. After a few minutes of watching our position, Ed signals me to return to the cockpit.

"Is that anchor set or not? We need some animals for next week's lab!" Ed cries above the noise of the wind. I point astern at the way the dinghy bucks in the waves. Maybe a professional athlete could jump into the dinghy without crashing into *Velella*, falling overboard, or sinking the dinghy, but not even a master mariner could make the hundred yards or so to shore without flipping the dinghy over in the waves. "It's too much, Ed. We should quit." I hesitate to disagree with him, but both Ed and I know that I am correct. "Maybe so. Let's just give it another minute or two."

While waiting for a miraculous change of weather, lunch seems to be a good idea. In the shelter of the cabin, the wind abates and I make up sandwiches for both of us. The lettuce on my sandwich, however, escapes as soon as I set the plate up on deck. It blows like a tumbleweed across the wave tops until it grows wet enough to stick to the water and soon sinks from view. Clearly, it is time to head back in. Looking at the clock, we realize that it is past time for dead low tide, and the wonderful flat has never broached the surface. Ed suggests that the wind is blowing in so hard from offshore that the sound never fully emptied on the outgoing tide, leaving the sandflat submerged.

Trying to raise the anchor is an exercise in effort, speed, and pure terror for a few moments. Since the current reversed, it is now aligned with the wind direction, and we face directly into both. I pull in the chain against their combined force, struggling with the full weight of the boat against the rode, until just at the critical moment, the windlass jams. I have apparently broken us free from the bottom because we start to rapidly drift toward the shallow lee shore, but Ed doesn't dare run too hard with the engine while we are still trailing the anchor rode behind us. Finally, in desperation, I jerk on the rode with all my might, and a surge of adrenaline from the fast-approaching lee shore provides me with the strength to break loose the knot, the chain fairly flies onto the deck as I pull it in, and the anchor appears from the depths.

Signaling to Ed that the anchor is in, I notice his worried look change to relief as we turn sharply and head directly for the channel. As I straighten up and look astern, I see the source of his worry; while I was struggling with the anchor rode, we were being pushed rapidly toward the shoal. "Whew," I comment as I return to the cockpit for the ride home, "since we couldn't get ashore with the dinghy, I thought we'd try collecting on that flat directly from *Velella*!"

On the very next day, the same trip is much more benign. Instead of fighting nature, we wait until it meets our needs. We sail easily out to the sandflat on a warm, sunny day with a gentle breeze blowing, pause for a leisurely lunch while waiting for the flat to appear, then row the dinghy ashore across calm waters.

On this pleasant trip, the sandflat is fairly paved with sand dollars. Most of them are dead, and I collect their perfectly white, circular skeletons as presents for friends and family. The living animals are grayish-brown, and each dollar hosts a pair of tiny crabs that live on its underside. These crabs are the smallest species of crab, and they live only with sand dollars. Like a remora on a shark or a pet dog under the table, the crabs survive by eating the small bits left over from the dollar's meal.

The living sand dollars, when I pick them up from the beach, wiggle their small spines until I set them down again. Their crab pair scurries around its host, then drops off the rim of its body like rats leaving a sinking ship. As soon as I replace the dollars on the sand surface, their tiny spines push aside the sand and they slowly sink from view. Soon they are invisible, nothing more or less than a smooth place in the sand, effectively hidden from other prying eyes and beaks.

Although the sand dollars are alive, they don't seem alive the way we often think of animals. Instead of flailing arms and legs, only their tiny spines move as they desperately try to escape the hands that clutch them. They are voiceless, too, unable to cry out against their capture. Still, they struggle in their own way, they try to escape, and they feel the pain of death. They are alive. Too often these living animals, which are covered in a soft gray velvet, are collected by unknowing or uncaring people, set out to die a slow death in the sun as their tiny spines and reddish tube feet wave fruitlessly and forlornly, then tossed into the trash or a bucket of bleach when they begin to smell of death and decay.

As I stand here with my feet awash in the ocean water, I can hear the voice of the sand dollar. It is a small voice, quiet and soft, hard to hear unless you know how to listen. The ocean's voice is loud and deep as its surf pounds the beachhead like rumbling tympani. A laughing gull calls from overhead, high and shrill, a lingering note. If I move my foot, the sand grains crunch beneath me, adding their voices to that of the ocean and the animals. The ocean is full of voices: cries of death and cries of birth, cries of pleasure and those of pain. My voice is somewhere in that mix, part of the whole, the song of the salt marsh.

Ed and I leave our dinghy at the ocean's edge and walk toward higher ground. There, a phalanx of fiddler crabs confronts us. Like a company of soldiers, they march down the beach until we advance, and then as a unit they retreat toward the protective marsh grass, where their burrows are located. There are so many in one location that they produce an eerie, hollow, almost mechanical noise as countless legs clack against thousands of bodies. It is barely, but distinctly audible, a constant and low-level rasping like a sound suited to a nightmare. While we herd them back and forth, they warily watch with claws folded next to their bodies. Only much later, after we have nearly forgotten them and no longer pose a threat, do they begin the display for which they are famous. The males, with either their right or left claw grossly enlarged, wave this badge of their masculinity both to intimidate other males and to entice the even-handed females into their burrows.

On the muddier side of the flat, hundreds of tiny horseshoe

crabs, none larger than a quarter, plow through the mud. Instead of nice, straight rows, however, their furrows curve left and right, overlapping or crossing one another crazily. Only a horde of drunken plowmen or an animal without a human sense of order could have created such wild interlacings. The tiny crabs are the new year's recruits, freshly hatched from the millions of eggs their parents laid a few weeks ago.

Amazingly, these ancient animals, which have withstood uncountable challenges over millions of years, are now in decline all along the eastern seaboard. The number of individuals is decreasing dramatically. Overfishing is partly to blame, for huge numbers of the adults are collected as bait by fishermen and by the medical industry. Their blood contains compounds that cannot be reproduced in the lab yet are important medically, so adult crabs are collected, held in tanks, and periodically bled. Sylvia Earle, in *Sea Change*, describes how fishermen collect only the egg-bearing females, killing them for eel bait, and thus decimate the population by removing the very eggs that could recover it. Climate change is also causing problems as waters warm and kill more larvae. In yet another example of the symbiotic interactions in ecosystems, migratory shorebirds are declining along with the crabs. Red knots, among other migratory shorebird species, depend on the eggs of horseshoe crabs as food during their migration from pole to pole. As fewer crabs lay fewer eggs, fewer birds survive migration to lay their own eggs.

While thoughtlessly following tracks of the tiny crabs, I suddenly realize that I am standing in a dense concentration of them. Unable to see a clear path through them, my feet are rooted to the spot. Aware of them now, I cannot mindlessly crush the newborn, ancient animals with each footstep. I wonder how I will ever get clear of them. Finally, I just remove them all from one foot-sized area, step onto it, then clear another area ahead of me to step onto. The ancestors of these very horseshoe crabs had been crawling onto a mudflat just like this one long before the footprint of humanity had been impressed upon the Earth. The crabs were abundant when Europeans arrived and are pictured in John White's drawings of America from 1585.

A laughing gull swoops out of the sky to pick up a small crab, crushing it in its beak. Landing so gently on the beach that it leaves no footprint, the gull throws back its head to swallow the tender morsel. The millions of eggs laid by the adult crabs are needed to replace all those consumed by other hungry animals, in the natural circle of life that has been turning for millions of years. In the biological reality of recycling and rebirth, these molecules that I see as juvenile horseshoe crabs are being transformed as I watch into molecules of gull. The point at which one stops and the other begins is unidentifiable and ultimately, without meaning, since generation is a process, not an end point. As Mary Oliver has written in her "Poem of the One World":

> This morning
> the beautiful white heron
> was floating along above the water
>
> and then into the sky of this
> the one world
> we all belong to
>
> where everything
> sooner or later
> is part of everything else
>
> which thought made me feel
> for a little while
> quite beautiful myself.

Wandering across the mudflat, looking for indications of organisms living there, is much like wandering down the beach hunting for shark's teeth. As a child, I would walk slowly for hours, face bent toward the sand, searching intently for the shiny black triangles of teeth. Hundreds now lie piled in a dozen different lamp bases and cuplike halves of large shells, artifacts of my travels. Absorbed in my focus on beach sand, I became lost in the moment, my concentration unbroken. Just red sand, white sand, shell fragments, then a quick strike with my fingertip and a small black speck, half-buried under debris, comes to light as a magnificent, perfect tooth. Again and again, hour after hour, I focused on the patterns of beach sand.

Like the beach of shark's teeth, this beach, too, is no clean sterile world, but a habitat full of animals. By knowing their habits, they become visible everywhere. Small craters left by feeding activities, piles of defecated sand or small pellets of organic matter, and tracks left by their travels are the clues to their presence. In order to see, you must first learn what to look for.

Down near the lowest extent of the tidewater, I find a burrow that differs from all the others I have seen. The clean hole is about the width of a pencil. Unlike the other burrows, it lacks an enormous pile of sand coiled up like soft-serve ice cream, there are no fecal pellets like chocolate jimmies to decorate it, and no feeding cone or crater is associated with it. Ed pounces with the shovel, slicing into the sand as if parting it with a broadsword. Most burrowing animals are faster than a slow and deliberate shovel stroke; only lightning-quick shovels, or bird beaks, can cut off their rapid retreat into the sediment. The shovelful of that creature's world separates from the beach as Ed gently raises the shovel and deposits the sand in the sieve. I take the sieve to the water's edge, and with a few dunks into the ocean's water, sieve away the sand and mud, leaving the animal exposed to the sunlight.

It is a sea cucumber, an animal related to sand dollars and one I feel a fondness for. Another sea cucumber species, similarly delicate and transparent, was the focus of my doctoral research. Each time I see one I am reminded of the pleasures of being a student: asking endless questions, searching for answers, learning enough to ask more questions. There is really no difference between a professor and a student, except that professors get to teach some of what is known while learning some of what is not yet known. My graduate advisor told me that as long as I was just one lecture ahead of my students, I would make it. He's right. Even barely ahead of them, I'm still their instructor, and have discovered that I enjoy teaching them about these fabulous animals. The profession of teaching is perhaps best expressed as a love of learning. There are opportunities to experience learning even while teaching others.

I'll never forget the day during my college career, studying for an upcoming exam no less, when I realized that I could do what I love to do and make a profession of it. I could study, work, read, learn, and attempt to understand life. There are so many mysteries we do not understand, and others that we do understand, but incompletely. How does a fragile monarch butterfly leave a flower in Toronto, Canada, and alight on a tree branch in central Mexico? How does a single egg cell give rise to a complex, multicellular organism with all its components and systems in the correct location? Why do so many animals that live in the oceans, some of the very ones we were collecting, go through a life stage that differs so radically from the adult that the relationships between many adults and their larval stages are unknown? All these questions have very practical implications for humans, whether they are the improvement of navigation systems or the control of developmental processes, but they are also basic fundamental questions to understand how nature works. How can we understand the world we live in and the rules we live by unless we study the other organisms with whom we exist? We can only make new discoveries and come to new understanding when we ask those questions that begin with "why" and "how" and are allowed the latitude to search in all directions. And studying these animals, seeing them in their natural habitat, observing their relationship to the environment and to each other is a good place to begin.

So this day we spend collecting some of the animals that inhabit the edge of the sea in order to study them and, perhaps, place one more piece in life's giant puzzle. Some days I feel as if I hold the piece, prepared to place a key part of the whole picture, and some days I feel as if someone else is holding me, the piece, and wondering where to place it. I am connected to the other biologists who came before me and those who may come after. I see a pattern because someone many years ago placed together a few key pieces and left that portion of the puzzle finished. Now I can build on what that person accomplished and leave a little more of the pattern deciphered.

We are all products of the totality of our experiences, both learned and inherited, beginning our lives with the legacy of what our parents and ancestors gave to us. At a bare minimum, they provide us with the foundation of who we are in our genetic heritage. We start there. We are influenced by our genes, which code for the building blocks and the inherited patterns of our bodies and minds. As such, genes describe the range of possibilities we each have available to us. If my hair is dark because my parents' hair is also dark, it should be no surprise that I also share an interest in science with them.

But nature is only what we start with. Nurture matters too. Because I showed a natural aptitude in science, it was encouraged and I learned much more about it. Learning engenders more study, which results in more learning. I had the luxury of a formal education available to me, and I pursued it to its climax. Beginning with my genetic heritage, I built on what I enjoyed and had the freedom to explore. Even with this same set of genes, had I been born in a different time or place that, for example, placed no value on female scientists or had no sandbanks to explore, the course of my life would differ.

Ultimately, then, it is our environment, both cultural and biological, that determines who we become. In addition to the collective knowledge inherited from our forebears in oral traditions, libraries, and artwork, we also learn from the complex and nurturing natural communities in which we live. And if that milieu is so important in shaping us, then what does it mean for our children that we are creating depauperate biological systems? Biological diversity is in decline around the world. We have lost and are losing species, individuals, and even whole communities, already the equivalent of burning several libraries of Alexandria. Today's children won't see the same natural world that I have seen. We've saved some species from extinction, like ospreys and pelicans and alligators. We've even increased the numbers of some individuals, such as ring-billed gulls. But I wonder how much longer the manatees in Florida will survive, or the right whales that live offshore, or the red knots that depend on horseshoe crab eggs.

Not only have we damaged the environment that nurtures us, but we even affect our very nature. By poisoning our environment with chemicals that affect our reproduction and development, we damage our genetic heritage as well. And that limits what we can do in the future. Children today carry loads of chemicals that affect their ability to learn and to think clearly, as described by Theo Colburn in *Our Stolen Future* and elsewhere. Permanently decreased intelligence, nonrecoverable through more than a decade of education, was shown in children whose mothers ate a high proportion of contaminated fish. Defects in intellect are harder to identify than hypospadias, cancer, or asthma, but all have been linked to environmental poisons.

We haven't collected enough data to determine whether the overall biodiversity of sedentary animals of the sea floor has been reduced. Ed and I find many different species on our collections so that the number of species seems unimpaired. We can still locate the animals we expect to find on our mudflats over the twenty years or more we've been collecting them. But our best mudflats are relatively isolated and in undeveloped areas. In other places, such as Florida Bay, Tampa Bay, or Chesapeake Bay, sedentary animals are clearly in decline.

When oil spills occur, we see images of pitiful birds and dolphins, killed or injured by the oil. We see fish kills and hear about the horrible burdens placed on the fishermen whose livelihoods have been affected. But the small animals on the seafloor receive no press. They are eliminated by the sludge that falls on them, suffocated in their burrows. Unlike the birds, fish, and mammals that we empathize with, these sediment-dwelling animals cannot swim and therefore cannot move away.

They are, however, at the base of the food chain, supporting the lives of those very birds, fish, and dolphins. When we kill the animals on the bottom, we pull them out of the ecosystem, and the larger animals have less food. Fewer fish can survive if their food resources, these sediment-dwelling creatures, are less abundant.

It is easy to understand that less food means fewer animals higher up the food chain, but that is not the only problem. When we allow chemicals to build up in the sediments to levels that are unhealthy but not necessarily deadly, we set up biomagnification of poisons just as we have done on land. Rachel Carson recognized the initial problems visible on land, but she also understood their potential hazard in the sea. In the sea, it is more difficult to see the effects until they reach enormous levels. Now they have.

Huge dead zones exist in the world's oceans, and not only from oil spills and chemical contamination. At the mouths of many large rivers, such as the Mississippi, the James that empties into Chesapeake Bay, and the Neuse that drains the commercial heart of central North Carolina, dead zones have been created by the efflux of waste from our cities and farmlands. Excess nutrients, produced when fertilizers run off, sewer systems leak, and animal waste accumulates, all run downhill to the sea. The nutrients added to the water cause algae to grow, which sounds innocuous, but the algae grow prolifically and die off quickly. Once dead, they form mats that decompose slowly, and decomposition uses up all the available oxygen in the water. Dead zones aren't just devoid of fish; they are devoid of life. Nothing can live in sediments that lack oxygen.

Estuaries, such as the Mississippi Delta, the Chesapeake Bay, and Pamlico Sound, are incredibly important ecological and economic areas. They are the nursery grounds for most of our commercially important fish and shrimp. They are the only places we capture blue crabs, oysters, and crayfish. When we allow estuaries to become polluted dead zones, we are endangering all these animals and the people who depend on them for their livelihood. And do we really want to eat fish that carry "just a little bit" of contaminants? When dolphins die from biomagnification of pollutants, we should be concerned, because dolphins eat at the same level on the food chain as we do. They are not the only animals in danger.

The sea cucumber we collect from the mudflat is beautiful. Its skin is transparent and covered with white sparkles, which are miniscule hooks shaped like old ship's anchors. It sticks to my hand like Velcro as I turn it upside down, the tiny hooks unnoticeable, but set resolutely in my skin. Its body is so delicate that I am careful when removing it from my hand; if it remained stuck fore and aft and was pulled too hard, it would break in the middle. It is adapted not to human hands, but to holding onto the walls of its protective burrow. This animal may not have seen sunlight since its wandering, swimming, larval form found the shovelful of mud on which to settle down and call home. Sea cucumbers and other animals like it depend on the current to distribute their larvae into new locations.

Many species entrust their very eggs to the rhythms of the sea and never leave their burrows. To reproduce, they send up a small portion of their bodies above the sediment to release their gametes into the sea. Their entire life cycle is solitary: once egg meets sperm, development proceeds as the embryo becomes a larva, the larva finds its own way, feeds itself, and survives until it locates a suitable home, then settles down and grows into an adult that will, at some point, release sperm or eggs.

Like any good gambler, however, these sedentary animals have a few tricks to improve their chances, and perhaps the most common phenomenon, whether the animals live buried in sediment or glued to a coral reef, is a synchronous release of eggs and sperm. Although the females and males never make direct contact with one another, the warming water and lengthening days trigger the maturation of their gametes. The cue that signals the release of the gametes into the water is usually the phase of the moon. For example, the corals on Australia's Great Barrier Reef expel eggs and sperm simultaneously on a single night or two each year. Divers report that the billons of cells actually discolor the water, leaving an oily slick on the surface and a fertile aroma on the air.

Another shovelful of sand in the sieve reveals the front end of an acorn worm, a rarely studied animal closely related to the chordates, the phylum of animals to which we belong. Big, barely moving worms that live buried in sandy mud, they constantly swallow mud, absorb the useful material, and defecate coiled piles of sand that may be as large as a German shepherd's droppings—hardly the picture of what we think of as a relative! Only by studying the details of their structure did their relationship to chordates become known. They have precursors to all the major components of a chordate, such as neural tubes and nerve cords. Some of these details are strikingly similar, but curiously different to chordate structures. What other secrets do these creatures hold? What new directions might we travel if only we could understand them better?

One reason they are rarely studied is because it is so hard to catch a whole one. They can be six feet long and very fragile, unsuited to coarse probing by a shovel, but luck is with us. After unearthing two different worms as though they were priceless fossils, carefully brushing away sand with my fingertips, I stop to look carefully at them. One is gray and swollen, full of eggs, and the other, with a whitish cast to its skin, is a male. With a little more luck, we may have both the larvae and adults to study.

These animals have an independent swimming larva, clear as glass, that lives a life completely different from the adult. Although the huge wormlike adult lives buried in muddy sediment, the tiny bell-shaped larva swims and feeds in the plankton. The two look nothing alike and, for all practical purposes, might as well be distinct species, but they are not, for given the right conditions, the larva settles to the bottom and transforms into the adult, much as a caterpillar metamorphoses into a butterfly. How is such a transformation controlled? Why is such drastic metamorphosis required?

How much of the larval body is really different from the adult, and how much is actually the same? There is so much to learn!

Our luck holds, for we return to Ed's laboratory and set up the acorn worms in a tank with sand and seawater. They immediately spawn, and within hours we have transparent larvae. Ed feeds them a little food coloring mixed in water, and documents the flow of water through the larva's body. With a graduate student, he shows that an enigmatic larval organ of previously unknown function is a precursor to the adult kidney. We know more, now, not only about the form and function of the larvae, but about the adults, too, because we can link the kidney formation in the larva with that of the adult.

As inevitably as day and night, or sun and moon, the tide turns and begins its movement back up the sandflat. Slowly at first, then with increasing speed, footsteps are erased by the water's encroachment on the temporary land. Water trickles into holes left behind by our shovel until the small stream of water erodes away the edges of the hole and the sides collapse as water rushes in from many different directions. The animals buried in the sandy mud are covered again by the life-giving sea. The horseshoe crabs left exposed to gulls by the retreating tide are embraced by the rising water and the predatory stingrays that will come with it.

We reluctantly abandon our explorations as the sea reclaims its ownership. As I stand in knee-deep water beside the small dinghy, a pod of dolphins cruise just offshore. Soon they will be swimming here where I have spent the last hour walking. This bit of the world is both land and sea; it is defined by their union. Our professions, too, are both the way we make a living and the way our lives acquire meaning. Pleasure comes from this union, from the realization that our work can be rewarding, fulfilling, and just plain fun. I feel confident that I've picked the right profession, one that supports me not just monetarily, but philosophically.

The Lowcountry of
South Carolina

HEADING DIRECTLY OUT OF PORT ROYAL SOUND TO SAIL an offshore passage might seem like an invigorating return to our cruise, but when I awake on the morning of our planned departure in a black mood, any pleasant prospect for the day dissipates into the cool morning air. Ed is excited and ready to get under way, for he has spent the entire previous day climbing around the boat so that we would be prepared for the next leg.

Inlets make me uncomfortable, and I dislike discomfort. Rather than face my own fear of grounding, hitting a shoal, losing steerageway, being swept overboard into the sea, or sinking the boat, I just stew. It takes me twice as long as it should to pull the covers off the sails, then longer still to stow them. I find endless items below decks that need securing. Returning from my second trip to the marina's bathroom, I find Ed pacing the deck, the engine already rumbling smoothly to assist in our pull away from the dock.

"Okay, toss those docking lines aboard!" he calls, enthusiastic about the sail but frustrated by my delay. "Come on! What's taking you so long?"

"I don't want to go. Let's just spend one more day at the dock."

"And do what?" Ed sits down abruptly, nearly collapsing at the helm. He swiftly cuts the engine off with a sharp twist of the key.

"Jennifer," he says, "if you didn't want to go you should've just said so, up front, instead of dawdling around this morning and wasting so much time. If you don't want to sail, that's fine, but tell me so that I can do something else. I've wasted over an hour this morning getting ready. Now I'll have to undo everything. Another wasted hour."

"Okay," I say, taking a deep breath and facing up to my fear. "I'm sorry I ruined the day. I'm worried about the inlet. It frightens me, and with this wind up like it is, the inlet passage will be rough. I was afraid to go out this morning. I should've just said so. I'm sorry."

He looks up at me then. His voice is soft. "I know. I wondered why you were acting so strangely this morning. Then I realized it was the sail. You didn't want to go. I was looking forward to it, after all the work I did yesterday on this thing." He gestures to the engine. "It's okay. We don't have to go if you don't want to. But why do we just sit here at the dock when we own a sailboat and the wind is blowing?"

Perhaps a compromise is in order. After all, it is silly to be worried about a little wind. But when I really pause to consider, it is actually the passage through the inlet that is bothering me, not the wind. We've had a couple of rough experiences in Charleston Harbor, when the tide and wind were opposed, pushing up a nasty chop that left me feeling weak and pounded. "What about this, Ed? If the wind holds, we can raise sail as soon as we pass the bridge. It will take an hour or two to get through Port Royal Sound and we can sail the whole way. But instead of going out the inlet, we could keep on the waterway. What do you think?"

Ed looks up from where he is sitting and turns the key back on. "I think it's a good compromise." So we leave for Georgia, but stay along the Intracoastal Waterway instead of heading offshore.

We knew almost nothing about sailing when we bought *Velella*, but she wasn't the first sailboat that Ed and I sailed together. Our first sail was really the beginning of our relationship. One of Ed's friends kept a sailboat on a deep, clear mountain lake in western South Carolina. When his friend, Karl, invited Ed for a sail one afternoon, Ed asked if he could bring me along. What a test of a new relationship!

We set off on a beautifully crisp spring day, with a hint of ice still in the air. The sun was bright and warm, though, with promises of summer. I snuggled down into the cockpit, bundled up inside a sweater. Karl shouted instructions forward to Ed from the cockpit, steering with a small outboard motor while Ed raised the sails. I had nothing to do but watch and sip on a steaming mug of hot chocolate.

The wind filled the sails as we cleared a wooded point. The boat heeled over sharply. Unprepared, I was tossed out of my comfortable position and came up hard against the coamings on the starboard side. About half the hot chocolate dumped on me and the other half on the deck, but I kept the mug in hand.

Laughing gently, but moving quickly, Ed returned to the cockpit. "You weren't ready for that, now, were you?" Karl looked embarrassed until I laughed too. I imagined that I did look funny. In a quick second, I changed from elegant yachtswoman sipping hot chocolate to naïve young boater who couldn't anticipate a breath of wind. The image I had created of myself was shattered. "You'll have to try harder than that to knock me overboard," I said to them both. "Looks like I'm on a steep learning curve!"

I was, too. In the few hours we sailed on the lake that afternoon, I learned to steer with a tiller, douse and raise sails, and handle the jib sheets on a tack. The tiller was the hardest for me because it required that I push the tiller away from the direction that I wanted the boat to go. When I wanted to turn to port, I pulled the tiller to starboard. When I wanted to turn to starboard, I pushed the tiller to port. I was never quite sure that I was doing the right thing until the boat began to turn, either the way I had hoped, or not. As a result, steering was not my favorite job. I didn't want to look too foolish in front of those two men, especially the one that seemed destined for me.

Handling the sails was different. I was confident and strong. I loved standing by the mast and raising or lowering the sails as fast as I could once the helmsman gave me the signal. Usually, just a nod and shout of "Okay!" when we faced dead into the wind, and up or down I'd haul the sails. It was muscular work, but exhilarating. I could feel the blood pouring through my veins as I pulled the halyards.

Those sails were our wings. Around the docks, a flock of mallard ducks bobbed lazily as they waited for handouts from boaters. When they took to wing, just as when the wind filled our sails, grace, beauty, and power suddenly emerged from a rather mundane presence. I longed for that feeling of transformation from the ordinary just as I loved the freedom to fly before the wind.

Exhilarated and exhausted, we returned to the dock after a few hours of that initial sail. My leg muscles quivered from being constantly contracted as my legs were braced against the cockpit, and Ed's arms were sore from holding the tiller, but we sat up most of the night as we talked about our shared experience. "Do you realize we've spent hours racing around without burning any gas, without even walking? All we did was hold up a piece of cloth," Ed was saying to me as I thought along similar lines. So simple a device, such a pure and present sensation, such a connection to the past and sailing ships that crossed oceans. We were both giddy from all the stimulation of the day.

We talked there like two old salts, analyzing each aspect of the day's sail. "I think we could've gotten more speed out of her if we'd kept the jib flatter," or "When the wind came up so strong in the late afternoon, we could've taken in a reef and she'd have been easier to handle." Finally, though, we came back to the beauty of it all. Moving around over the lake's crystalline surface, the Blue Ridge Mountains reaching up in the distance, shores clad with green extending right down to the water's edge, yet with nothing but the wind to propel us around. No fossil fuels, no engines, no noise, just fabric and air.

"Let's buy a sailboat!" he said that evening, after we'd exhausted ourselves discussing the sail. Asking someone to buy a sailboat is a little like buying a house together, and we weren't married at that point. Shocked at his suggestion, I was even more astounded to hear myself reply, "Well, what's available?"

We quickly found a small boat for sale that was docked at the same marina as Karl's boat, and took it for a glorious introductory sail. I took a deep breath, and we bought the boat that spring. By late summer, we were married.

On our very first sail on that reflective surface, a soaring, red-tailed hawk followed us. It flew effortless circles overhead while we adjusted our sails to take advantage of the wind. As we approached the steep shoreline of a partly drowned mountain, the hawk caught the updraft of wind that the mountainside deflected, and it soared upward, nearly out of sight. We tacked into the wind and turned back the way we'd come, but angled farther down the lake. The angle we traveled put us into a protected cove, and we made one last turn into the now failing wind, with just enough steerageway to position ourselves in the center of the cove, then tossed over the anchor. We were alone in a beautiful spot. A tiny islet and shallow bank around it formed a protective corner of the cove, leaving only the main opening deep enough to sail through. The verdant hillsides flowed gently toward the greenish-blue water of our little cove.

Although it really wasn't hot enough to justify a swim, neither was it cold enough to stop us, and we slipped overboard into the inviting water. Its coolness, however, encouraged us to swim, and we made toward the near shore of the islet. In a few strokes, we closed the distance and climbed ashore. We emerged from the lake onto land, and within minutes circumnavigated the islet on foot, stumbling through shallows or carefully traversing solid land. Waves and wakes of boats eroded the land face that met the main body of the lake, and the steep bank dropped abruptly into water. Exposed roots twisted at crazy angles, pointing like gnarled fingers from the red subsoil, and in shallows beneath the bank, clods of red clay piled high.

Ancient rhododendrons and craggy mountain laurel clung to the steep side, but on the gentler slope of the islet that faced the cove, we came upon a blooming moccasin flower, a native orchid. It glowed there in the late-afternoon sunshine of spring, a pink jewel hidden among green gems of leaves. As we swam back to our boat, I opened my eyes while underwater and thought I could see pale, pink rocks on the bottom of that drowned landscape, ghosts of long-dead flowers. How many must have been submerged by the waters of this reservoir.

A few days later, hiking along a leafy trail, we came across another pink beauty and stopped to admire it. A bumblebee climbed over the swollen pink lip, looking for a way inside, hopeful of finding a nectar reward. But the beautiful flowers provide neither nectar nor pollen for insects to consume; instead the flower uses the bee to transport its pollen in two sticky sacs that adhere to the bee's head or back. Still, some bees are slow to learn, visit another moccasin flower, and unintentionally deliver the load of pollen to fertilize the seeds, all without receiving nectar in return. Ed wrote a poem for my birthday:

TIME LAPSE

Before, and since, first footfalls on moss,
Moccasin flowers buckled the leafy mat,
And rose, blushing, into the dawn.

Seeing one, the humble bee's kiss
Parts lips; slipping in, restless
To avoid being lost in flower.

Reflection from a distant bloom
Glints on that mosaic eye,
Pleading for renewed embrace.

Thus fulfilled, the union complete,
A puff of dust, a flash of wings,
Flight into light.

William Bartram traveled through the Carolinas in the 1770s. Like John Lawson, he was a collector and naturalist who explored the region and recorded his observations of plants, animals, and Native peoples, and his book, now called *Travels of William Bartram*, is still in print. Andre Michaux, another naturalist, followed Bartram a decade later. Among his many significant finds, near the headwaters of the Keowee River, Michaux collected a rare evergreen plant known as Oconee bells, whose attractive shiny leaves resemble those of *Galax*. Michaux's specimen, however, was not in flower, and his discovery triggered a one-hundred-year botanical search for the holy grail of a second specimen in flower, which was finally rewarded in 1877 with the flower's rediscovery.

It is worth the effort to see the flower. Five white, fringed petals surround five lemon-yellow, shield-shaped stamens and a pink central stigma. The flowers are not only stunning, but are welcomed as one of the earliest spring-blooming wildflowers. The emotional response of mountaineers to this harbinger of spring is captured elegantly in the song "Acony Bell," written and performed by the folksinger Gillian Welch.

Reservoirs like the one we sailed on were built as hydroelectric projects, reducing the use of coal to produce electricity, but they are not without environmental effect. For example, Michaux's original collection site of Oconee bells is now drowned by Lake Jocassee. The Native American towns that both men visited are similarly engulfed. The biological community is destroyed; the historical sites inaccessible.

Within a few short months, we had explored many hidden coves, sailed deeper reaches of the lake, and dreamed of larger landscapes. Along with larger landscapes, though, came the thought of a bigger boat. "We could begin by sailing just in the Southeast and Caribbean," Ed said. "We could spend years exploring there. Imagine dropping anchor in crystal-clear water and diving over to catch a lobster for dinner, or anchoring in the middle of salt marsh and dragging in a cast net full of shrimp and blue crabs. And we could go anywhere in the whole world! Tahiti, Bali, Greece, just imagine the possibilities!"

It was so seductive, especially on a dreary winter day: to go anywhere that had a coastline; to be free to explore and free to stay as long as it took; to travel the same routes mariners had traveled for hundreds or thousands of years; to see some of the watery expanses of Earth. How could I say no? And so our search began, culminating in our purchase of *Velella* and now our exploration of the waters and marshes along the southeastern coast.

Although the inlets are usually rough, once offshore, sailing is just as interesting and pleasurable as traveling through salt marshes inshore. Offshore sailing is easy in that there are neither channel markers to follow without ceasing, nor are there many other boats to worry about, and it is relaxing because there is no constant attention to depth or fear of going aground as there is in the shallow ICW. It is faster, too, because of the continual, night-and-day sailing and because the route is more direct. There are no meanders along river courses or deviations around islands and shallows, and no close encounters with loaded barges. On the other hand, the ICW is comfortable, with the opportunity for regular meals, a full night's sleep, and placid water that rarely raises stomach-churning waves. There is little chance for really rough conditions, and it is nearly impossible to get lost, but the greatest attraction of the ICW is the constantly changing vista with the potential for an interesting plant or animal just around the next bend of creek. That is what draws us back time and again—the opportunity to see, to experience, to learn something new.

Sailing is something more than the quickest way to get from one point to another. It is a challenge, both physical and mental. To achieve a balanced sail set, the boat nearly cruising on her own, wind and seas combined with boat and body, is simply beautiful. To move slowly through the water and suddenly realize that it is full of living animals, delicate jellies that yet hold the power to kill and consume a more evolutionarily advanced fish, is humbling. Cruising in the

Southeast also requires a sense of humor and, sometimes, of resignation, especially while sitting on a sandbar waiting for high tide to lift us free. Wait long enough, and conditions will change.

Traveling slowly along the ICW gives us plenty of time to observe the salt marsh and to study its formation. Salt marsh ranges all along the eastern seaboard, but is best developed through South Carolina and Georgia, from approximately Cape Romain in South Carolina to the division between Georgia and Florida at St. Marys Entrance. One reason it is so extensive in the region is the shape of the land. A huge shallow semicircle, like a shark bite out of the coastline, creates a funneling effect. As the tide rises, ocean water enters all along the wide mouth of the funnel but gets forced into a narrower and narrower throat. This concentration of water results in higher high tides (and lower low tides) along this region of coastline than immediately north or south. The tidal range through this area, which is called the Atlantic Bight, can reach eight feet between high and low tide, and the tidal current often runs two or more knots. In part because the huge tidal range floods and then frees a wide swath of coastline with salt water on each tidal cycle, the southeastern coast has salt marshes as wide as farm fields. Spartina is one of the few plants that can tolerate a twice-daily bath with salt water followed by exposure to hot, dry air and intense sunlight.

Numerous large rivers also discharge their contents into the Bight, and the supply of marsh-building sediment is greatest along this stretch of coast. In southern South Carolina, the Santee, Cooper, Ashepoo, Combahee, Edisto, Coosaw, Morgan, Beaufort, and Savannah Rivers all flow into a relatively short stretch of coastline. South of the Savannah River, the salt marsh is supplied by drainage from the coastal plain itself rather than from large rivers that reach into the mountainous foothills. At their mouths, the rivers form salt marsh deltas, each of which opens to the sea via an inlet, or, from the river's perspective, an outlet.

These rivers carry sediment from the eroding Appalachian Mountains and inland areas to the sea. The soils themselves are built of many different types of material such as topsoil, clay, and rock. Quartz, in particular, breaks down into particles of sand. Look in any mountain stream and you will find the initial products of erosion that may eventually become beaches.

These rivers also carry the names of the Native American tribes who once called their shores home. The rivers were a means of travel, provided food as fish and invertebrates, and formed the basis of the rich soils that supported their agricultural societies. Most lowcountry rivers were occupied by tribes who were among the first groups to experience the expansion of English settlements and even earlier contact with Spanish explorers. We know little about these Native tribes because they were decimated by disease, slavery, and warfare so early in the colonial era. We know more about other tribes, such as the Cherokee, who lived farther west and therefore survived the onslaught of Europeans a little longer, allowing time for those same Europeans to write down what they knew of the Natives.

Because so many rivers are now dammed, less sand reaches coastal beaches. The sand is trapped behind the dams instead of periodically flushing downstream to the coast. When coupled with rising sea level and natural migration of beachfronts from north to south because of the predominant longshore current, many coastal zones have problems with the loss of sand. There is not enough natural replenishment.

For example, the Santee and Cooper Rivers in South Carolina are dammed to form Lakes Marion and Moultrie. As the big lakes slowly trap and fill with sediment, Cape Romain grows ever-smaller because it is starved of sediment for renourishment. This region of the Cape is an important stopover point for migratory waterfowl, whose numbers have been declining. When the dams were originally constructed, all the flow from the Santee was redirected through the Cooper River and into Charleston Harbor instead of the natural outlet at Cape Romain. By funneling all the Santee's water and sediment into Charleston, the Cape became physically smaller, lower in nutrients, and higher in salinity. In 1985, the Army Corps of Engineers attempted to correct the mistake by building a bypass around the dams, which increased water flow down to the Cape through the Santee River, but much of the sediment is still trapped behind the dams.

Migratory fish have also been drastically affected by the installation of dams that prevent their reaching the headwaters of rivers during their spawning runs. Salmon have received a lot of press, mostly because they are big fish that are important for the commercial fishing industry, but smaller fish are affected too. They are lower on the food chain and important food sources for larger fish. Their smaller size makes it even more difficult for them to overcome the dams or to scale the fish ladders that have been put into place for the large fish that can jump from pool to pool up the face of the dam and so reach the other side.

While there are many species of fish that have been reduced in numbers by the construction of dams, shad are arguably one of the most seriously affected. Enormous shad runs used to occur every spring all along the eastern seaboard, from the rivers of the lowcountry to those in New England. All the way up into the mountains, a small tree is called "shadbush" because it blooms at the same time of the historically prolific shad runs. Not long ago, the fish were so thick in the rivers that they could be dipped from the water with nets. Shad, along with menhaden, are the fish that Natives taught the English colonists to use as fertilizer in order to grow their crops by putting a dead fish into each hole with the corn seeds. The fish were so abundant that they could be used to fertilize corn rather than eat them directly. But overfishing, river pollution, and dam construction have taken a heavy toll. In 1896, 22,000 metric tons of shad were documented in commercial landings, but now fewer than 900 tons are taken each year even with vastly improved equipment and a larger fleet of boats. Whole watersheds now lack these fish, so historically important that John McPhee devoted an entire book, *The Founding Fish*, to them.

In addition to sediment, these rivers also carry the pollutants that have washed into them from their watersheds. Any chemical that is spilled or sprayed onto the land eventually washes off, and where it washes to is the river and then to the sea. By the time the rivers reach their mouths, they are full of whatever they have acquired from the land that drains into them. In addition to pollutants, this includes nutrients from agricultural fertilizers, concentrated animal facilities, and sewage. Nutrients cause algae to grow, and when it dies, oxygen is consumed by the bacteria that decompose it, creating conditions of low oxygen in the rivers and estuaries. While the dead zones in the Mississippi and Chesapeake exist permanently, shorter-duration low-oxygen events occur regularly in many southeastern rivers. Most reported fish kills result not from a direct spill of chemicals but from low oxygen, typically occurring late in the summer when the warm water is already low in oxygen.

For too long, we have assumed that "the solution to pollution is dilution," but the amount and toxicity of pollutants have reached levels that the estuaries cannot flush away. Only relatively recently have we enacted laws restricting the discharge of sewage from commercial and pleasure boats and installed pump-out stations at marinas that move the sewage off the boats and into city sewage treatment. Antifouling paints applied to boat bottoms to prevent growth are often designed to flake off and end up in the sediments, but newer formulations are now less toxic. As the number of boats and boaters increase, their individual contributions to pollution must continue to decrease if we are to conserve the estuaries.

Because of regulations associated with the Clean Water Act, first signed in 1972, point-source discharges into rivers from industries, sewage treatment plants, and power plants are much cleaner than they were in the 1950s, when Wilma Dykeman included in her book *The French Broad* a chapter entitled, "Who Killed the French Broad [River]?" There she writes that "when we turned away from the spring at the edge of the kitchen yard and turned on the faucet in our porcelain sink, we turned off our interest in what came out of the spigot." The French Broad River and other rivers are cleaner now because we have agreed to regulate what can be dumped directly into them from pipes that discharge from buildings large and small even though the number of pipes has increased by tenfold or more. The regulations not only resulted in environmental protection, but in economic improvement because more industries can use cleaner water. The problem now comes from the watersheds themselves, from nonpoint sources, from the pollutants that are discharged onto the surface of the land and then picked up and washed into the rivers. Agriculture is the single-largest source of nonpoint discharge of nutrients from fertilizers and animal waste and of pesticides, but it is not the sole source; our lawns, golf courses, city streets, and boats are significant sources as well.

The salt marsh is one of the most productive ecosystems on Earth because it is constantly provided with sediments that wash in from upstream. Since it is transitional, neither fresh nor salty and constantly changing, it is stressful to animals and plants that come in from the ocean and those that invade from the land. For those few species that have adapted to this zone, the resources available to them are immense and competition is limited. Blue crabs, shrimp, oysters, and the marsh grass spartina reproduce rapidly and grow vigorously. Because these species grow rapidly and reproduce quickly, they replenish themselves quickly and provide abundant harvests that can be repeatedly collected. Shrimp and crab harvests remain stable, with the amount caught each year varying based on environmental conditions rather than harvest effort.

Oysters, however, are on the decline. While they should be abundant because of their rapid growth and reproduction, they face two serious obstacles. First, planktonic oyster larvae settle on old oyster shell. The vast oyster beds that once occupied most of the eastern estuaries are much smaller in size, which we know both from direct experience and also because of the huge mounds of shells left behind by the Native Americans in their middens. These enormous mounds attest to an almost unimaginable abundance of oysters. Such a vast resource is now a memory of the past. Oyster-shell recycling has become more common as we have realized that new oysters won't grow back unless the old oyster shell is replaced, and the creation of these man-made oyster beds may help to recover the oysters.

Not just the oyster beds, but even the individual oysters are smaller in size than they once were. Individual oysters can live a long time, have few natural predators, and grow in size every year. Shells collected from the middens of Native Americans are sometimes a foot long and similar in shape and size to a human foot. A normal, healthy oyster reef is mostly composed of "uprights," each a vertical column of oysters cemented together. The oysters are staggered from top to bottom along the upright, but each has its gape, or mouth, end directed upward. The shell around the gape is thin and razor-sharp, which discourages animals such as raccoons or bare-footed humans from walking on the reef. The upward growth of the uprights is also the means by which oyster reefs keep above the smothering mud, which is deposited in the marsh. Reefs that have been harvested by gear dragging across it lack uprights because the animals have been knocked over, which slows the growth of any that survive and threatens them with burial.

A typical oyster filters fifty gallons of water per day while separating its organic food, which it swallows, from the inorganic silt, which it spits back into the water. They are effective natural filters, cleaning the water of whatever it contains. Not only do oysters concentrate and swallow food, including bacteria, algae, and miniscule plants and animals, from an enormous volume of water, but they also unwittingly ingest chemical pollutants and viruses. What doesn't kill them outright is stored within their bodies for whoever consumes them next and so on up the food chain. What we dump into a river will potentially end up in the oysters and other filter feeders we eat from the estuary downstream.

Port Royal Sound, through which we are sailing, forms a large area of salt marsh because more than one river converges with another to spew their contents together into the sea through the same inlet. The sediment carried by these rivers forms a central island,

Parris Island, with a lengthy and shallow spit that extends like a tongue projecting from the mouth of the sound toward the open ocean. In order to clear the spit, the channel markers seem to lead completely out into the ocean before doubling back into the next river channel. Because the sound is so large, we have enough room to sail for a couple of hours with a favorable wind, and it really is beautiful to sweep gracefully along, adjusting the sails while simultaneously watching channel markers. I wish I could get over the initial fear that caused my morning panic; the anticipation of crossing the sound was worse than the actual event. In the present, it is fun. In the future, it seemed frightening.

Still embarrassed about my irrational fear, I scramble around the cabin with an idea in mind. Ed is steering and calls down to ask what I am doing. Finding the object of my search, I push in a tape of Jimmy Buffett songs and turn on the speakers in the cockpit. Soon we are singing along to our favorites. When "Prince of Tides" starts to play, I can hardly believe the irony. Dafuskie Island, just south of Hilton Head, is singled out in the song, and it is the island we are currently passing. The Buffett song is about the lowcountry and its conversion into the playground of the wealthy. Its past is erased as the land is re-created in a new form. Like Dykeman asking, "Who Killed the French Broad?" Buffett asks, "Who Killed the Prince of Tides?" He says, "How can you tell how it used to be when there's nothing left to see?" I suppose my answer is that we must rely on the stories that people tell each other about what the biology or culture "used to be."

History is written by those who survive, for better or worse. Discovering stories from the past and telling them to each other enriches our present because it creates an image for us to see in our minds if not in reality. Think of unbroken forests of longleaf pines and enormous cypress trees, filled with ivory-billed woodpeckers and Carolina parakeets. They lived along these rivers not so long ago, along with the people who turned those trees into dugout canoes and had done so for thousands of years. Adding history helps us to appreciate what we have and to mourn what we have lost.

The lowcountry of South Carolina has a history, both biological and cultural. The Native American people who once lived along its shores are mostly gone and forgotten, recalled only vaguely by place-names that seem a little unusual to the English-tuned ear. We can confront the realities of African slavery because the descendants of the people who were stolen from their homelands and forced to adapt to the new world are with us still today whereas very few descendants of coastal Native Americans survive. For African Americans, reconciliation is possible and ongoing. Most tribes of Native Americans, also enslaved and displaced, are now extinct, and their complex cultures persist as nothing more than place-names. Who were the Sewee, the Ashepoo, the Kiawah? More than an outpost, a river, an island. The coastal tribes were numerous and diverse. We have a few snippets of stories about them, but we occupy the lands that were once theirs without much thought for who they were, how they lived, or what they knew.

One of the most beautiful stretches of southeastern coastal waters is Calibogue Sound, the most southern sound in South Carolina. Salt marshes, low wooded islands, and even white sandy beaches along the distant shore rim the sound's waters. A lighthouse stands in the distance, where the ocean is barely visible. As we sail through the sound in the early afternoon, the wavelets slapping our hull are dancing with sunlight, their tops glittering like jewels. Here the ICW is a gentle and beautiful channel that runs along the southern side of a large marsh, then cuts immediately into a river. Because the ICW never approaches the sea at the mouth of the sound, the boat channel is well protected from ocean swells, and the sound itself doesn't seem as immense and empty as some of the others.

As we sail peacefully along, we are joined by a pair of acrobatic birds, swooping within inches of shrouds and lines without ever touching wingtips to boat. They fly with us for most of an hour,

darting among the rigging as if it isn't there. Confused by their behavior, we wonder if they are investigating our chimney-like dorade
vents that project up from the cabintop and sweep fresh air belowdecks, and assume they are chimney swifts. After watching for
several minutes, however, we finally realize that they are picking off
greenheads, a biting horsefly that is common in the marshes during the summer months. The greenheads had plagued us with fierce
bites since the sun had warmed the air and our canopy cover, where
dozens of the flies gathered.

Once we realize that the birds are not really interested in the
vents, we look at them more closely and recognize them as swallows
instead of swifts. Most are barn swallows, the most colorful of all the
swallows and the only local species of swallow with a long, deeply
bifurcated tail, which often nest under bridges and docks. They circle out over the marsh to capture the insects flying there, pick off a
few greenheads from our canopy, then perch on the boat rigging as
they wait for another swarm of insects to appear. A few birds lack
swallow tails, have squared-off tails instead, and are greenish rather
than purple. They are tree swallows. In the fall, tree swallows collect
in great flocks along the edges of the marsh and come swooping out
to investigate everything, or maybe just to fly. They often pass by
close enough to touch, supremely aware of their extraordinary flying
capabilities, and as they bank and turn, their brilliant green backs
and short tails glow with iridescence in the sun.

Chimney swifts are dark little birds with a fluttering, bat-like
flight. They are most visible in the late afternoon and toward dusk
rather than in the heat of the day. When they are about, their high-
pitched twittering comes from far overhead, and I look up to see
their dark, cigar-shaped, silhouetted bodies, with longish wings that
curve backward like scythes, a stubby, rounded head, and a short tail
that merges imperceptibly with the body.

It is so beautiful in Calibogue Sound that we decide to spend the
night rather than travel any farther. Just ahead, the channel widens

where the mouth of another creek empties into it. We edge easily into the nice deep hole and drop the anchor.

Since we have a few hours before dark, we set out to explore the beautiful anchorage with our little dinghy. We head up the enticing creek, following it deep into the marsh. After a while, I realize how similar the marsh looks in every direction. I begin to worry. Can we find our way back out? But Ed is undeterred—there have been no additional creeks feeding into the one we are running, so we should be able to turn around and follow the watercourse, like Ariadne's thread, out of the labyrinth and back to our boat. As we turn yet another bend, the view changes. We've reached the high marsh, and there is finally something other than spartina and dark water.

In the high marsh, a few plants other than spartina can grow. In nearing land, running away from the sea, seawater has become more diluted by the input of freshwater from the land. In the upper reaches of the high marsh, where the salty water only occasionally reaches, two similar-looking small trees, the groundsel tree and marsh-elder, occupy the transitional area between marsh and land. These bushes grow about fifteen feet in height and have small, thick leaves. The leathery leaves prevent the evaporation of water from within the leaf, allowing the tree to survive on small amounts of freshwater. Stunted cedar trees can also survive the occasional intrusion of salt water.

Since the high marsh receives fresh groundwater, plants more often associated with freshwater marsh can survive. We look for a place to beach our dinghy and get out to explore, but black needle rush presents its sharp-tipped leaves to jab any unwary animal, including us, that might attempt to force its way through the marsh. Just ahead, though, we find a stretch composed of salt meadow hay. It is a gentler, slimmer species of *Spartina*, apparently palatable enough to cattle that they consume this plant of the high marsh. In New England, salt hay was harvested in order to feed land-based cattle. Down south, we rarely have enough to make harvesting it worthwhile.

Even flowers occur in the high marsh. The tiny, purple flowers of sea lavender last only a few days, but the dried stalk with its flower heads persists into autumn, and at this time of year, both new flowers and old stalks are present. I am delighted to find a patch of sea oxeye daisies nodding their yellow heads to the gentle breeze, a few drops of water on the ground behind them. A Wordsworth poem, "To a Child. Written in Her Album," springs to mind:

> Small service is true service while it lasts:
> Of humblest Friends, bright Creature! scorn not one:
> The Daisy, by the shadow that it casts,
> Protects the lingering dew-drop from the Sun.

In another area of high marsh, lawn-like grasses give way to glasswort, whose thick, fragile green fingers of stems protrude from the surface sand. In the colonial era, people ate them as pickles and in salads, so I try one. It is a salty, crunchy sensation of taste, too intense to really be pleasurable, but probably acceptable as part of a salad. In the early spring, before crops were harvestable and when food supplies were lowest, the vitamin-rich greens were no doubt welcomed by English settlers and Native Americans alike.

The area where the glasswort is growing looks different from the rest of the marsh. The low-growing glasswort and other short grasses reach only a few inches in height, and they surround an area of sand where nothing is growing at all. It is a salt panne, where the salinity is too high for any plant to grow. Ironically enough, salt pannes of the high marsh are saltier than seawater even though the high marsh receives input of freshwater from the land. The salt pannes form by way of evaporation, when salty water of high spring tides occasionally submerges the flats. Pure water evaporates in the hot summer sun, leaving behind solid salts, and these salts are concentrated until the panne is flushed by another spring tide, weeks away, or by a summer thunderstorm.

We explore the salt panne and the rest of the high marsh, enjoying our ability to walk in the marsh without sinking into the ooze of pluff mud. But soon we return to our dinghy and trace our way back through the sea of spartina. The small area of high marsh can hardly compete with the endless acres of spartina that we encounter.

It is *Spartina alterniflora*, after all, that is so thoroughly a resident of the salt marsh. Spartina, like all other vascular plants, sucks up moisture from its roots. The roots of spartina, however, are immersed in salt water, and the plant has evolved a method of salt secretion in order to remove the salt from the water. Salt glands on the underside of its leaves allow excess salt to be secreted from water that the plant absorbs, and sparkling crystals of salt are often visible there. Spartina also takes advantage of dead tissue that penetrates into the sticky black mud. The mud is very low in oxygen and carbon dioxide, but the roots of the plant need these gases in order to function. Spartina solves that problem by having relatively rot-resistant tissues. The old roots and stems remain scattered throughout the mud. As they finally begin to rot, they do so first in the centers, creating a hollow snorkel tube into the mud. The gases can move from the air above through these tubes and penetrate to the living roots of the plants.

From the view of the dinghy, it is easy to see that spartina grows tallest along the edges of creeks that weave through the marsh. Those plants on the edge receive first shot at the nutrients being transported by the creek as it overflows into the marsh at high tide. The blades of spartina effectively slow the water as it moves from the creek into the marsh, causing the nutritious particles to settle out around the roots of the plants along the edge of the creek. Those plants along the creek edges are also the last ones to lose the water as it retracts back into the creeks during ebbing tides. They feel fewer stressful effects of evaporation.

Spartina is the anchor that holds the marsh together and the baffle that allows the marsh to expand. As the water slows around its roots, mud collects, forming more marsh that gets colonized by more spartina. It is a tight connection and an exercise in reciprocation. Spartina needs marsh in order to grow, but the marsh itself grows as a result of the presence of spartina.

A host of animals depends on spartina for food or shelter. Some animals, such as periwinkle snails, graze algae from the surface of spartina blades. Their small, white shells shaped like spinning tops festoon the marsh grass, moving up and down stems and leaves as the tide rises and falls, grazing like tiny cows on a vertical pasture. They are not avoiding the water itself, but the blue crabs swimming and scuttling in it below. Some blue crabs, however, exhibit a glimmer of intelligence when they shake the spartina stem, causing the periwinkles to drop into the water. The crabs then crack the shells of these fallen snails and eat them.

Other animals, such as fiddler crabs, wait until spartina dies and decomposes into tiny particles, then they sift the mud to find little nutritious bits. The crabs pick up the muddy mix, swish it around with their mouthparts to separate food morsels from sand, then spit back out a perfect sphere of mud. Mud balls decorate the surface of mudflats where fiddlers are feeding. When fiddlers are not out foraging en masse for food, they wait inside their burrows, whose entrances they blockade with mud against high tide and long beaks of ibis. At low tide, they emerge to feed.

Still other animals hide underneath decaying spartina stems, piled up along the high tide line. The wrack line shelters coffee-bean snails and saltmarsh beachhoppers, both small animals the color of mud, from the effects of summer sun. Raccoons know to forage along the wrack line, occasionally scoring a dead fish or crab, but almost certain to find tiny snails. As they push aside piles of spartina stems, pale beachhoppers explode like firecrackers from underneath the protective mat.

Whether a marsh wren building a nest among its tips or a saltmarsh mussel settling among its roots, these marsh animals are intimately connected to spartina and to the marsh itself. Animals of the salt marsh, just as its plants, both form the marsh and are formed by it. The mussels, anchoring among the spartina roots, add stability to the marsh. Once the mussels are consumed by raccoons or oyster-catchers, their empty shells become the nursery cradles of blennies or a bit of hard substrate on which other animals can grow. Clapper rails, nearly invisible as their narrow bodies slip between the blades of spartina because they are "as thin as a rail," flip over the dead shells to catch the sheltering blenny or crab that might be hidden there.

Marsh wrens nest in living spartina, but use dead grass strands to build their nests. During our afternoon of enjoying the marsh by dinghy, we see our first marsh wren nest. At every bend in the narrow creek, we scare up a fussing marsh wren, a little brown ball that flutters briefly above the tops of the marsh grass then drops again into the sea of green. Suddenly, I see a bird emerge from a brown mass of material—it is a nest. Once I point it out to Ed, we see them everywhere: round bundles of spartina blades almost the size of a grapefruit, with a small entrance hole on the side. Both living and dead blades are interwoven so that the nest appears to be nothing more than a clump of dead grass haphazardly entangled in living spartina. We passed hundreds, or thousands, before we learned to see them as carefully constructed nests, and of all those that we saw, perhaps only 10 percent actually contained young. The rest were dummy nests, built by male birds to help disguise the real one. If luck remained with the birds, hungry raccoons and rice rats would tire of opening false nests before reaching the single nest with its cargo of young.

The nests of marsh wrens are placed just above the level of high tide. In fact, an unusually high spring tide can submerge nests. Spring tides are those tides with the greatest amplitude or height between low and high tide in one cycle; they are followed by neap tides, which are low amplitude, with less difference between high and low water. They are called spring tides because they "spring" up, not because they occur in the spring season. They should, perhaps, be called moon tides, because they are correlated with the full and new moons, when sun, moon, and Earth are aligned and the combined pull of their gravity is greatest. Spring tides (and neap tides) occur about every two weeks, which means that marsh wrens, with a period of about two weeks of incubation and another two weeks until the young fledge, will experience at least one spring tide during the nesting cycle. If their nest with eggs or young is destroyed, they try again. A hurricane or other strong storm that hits during the breeding season can prematurely end the lives of many marsh wrens and other marsh-nesting animals. The population of wrens is usually depressed in the year that follows a breeding-season hurricane.

To be immersed all day in the nature of the salt marsh restores us. We appreciate the freedom to drop anchor in a secluded backwater and listen to the sounds of the marsh, undistracted by engines or other human-made noises that most people no longer even notice in their hurried lives. From the virtual reality of everyday life, we enter the true reality of nature. We return to the present, leaving the past and the future alone, to listen. Peacefully anchored in this remote spot, so quiet that every gentle breeze through the marsh grass is audible first as a low, distant murmur, next as immediate and individual whispers that bend each grass blade, then again as a fading, gentle hum, spartina becomes whisper grass, described enchantingly in the ZBS radio drama series *Ruby,* by Thomas Lopez. Listening, we hear the whispers of the marsh, and of each other.

Georgia

SAILING IN SALT MARSHES TAUGHT US TO APPRECIATE EACH moment as unique. Instead of going with a list of things to see, we learned to look and see what was offered. If one goes to the marsh with a goal of seeing a dolphin, a wood stork, an osprey, then the absence of those animals means you saw "nothing" on the trip. The only thing guaranteed in a salt marsh is marsh grass. Even water is sometimes there, sometimes gone.

Before we go "anywhere" the next morning, we notice jellies floating in the water alongside us. The creek is crowded with tiny cannonballs the size of a quarter, larger moon jellies the size of a dessert plate, and even a few unusual box jellies about two inches to a square side. We float there for an hour or more, lost in the present, dipping up jellies and putting them in buckets to see them better, pouring excess water back over the side. A boat comes out from a nearby marina to see if we are in trouble. We laugh together happily, enjoying our camaraderie as the puzzled captain, waved away, turns back to the marina.

Not all jellies have stings strong enough for us to detect. The cannonballs, for instance, are brownish-purple, tough jellyfish that do not sting. They use their short, stiff, rootlike tentacles to collect the plankton on which they feed. These small cannonballs we collect are juveniles, for adults get almost as large as a soccer ball. The small ones, called "jellyballs," are favored bait used by sheepshead fishermen. The bigger cannonballs, called "cabbageheads," wash ashore in the summer months, and their tough bodies are slow to disintegrate in damaging surf. If I happen to find them alive, still colorful and complete, I toss them back into the surf and wish them luck, though they are more than likely to wind up on the beach again.

The moon jellies, by contrast, are pale and delicate creatures, shaped more like a flattened plate than a ball, which collapse when the support of water is replaced by the less dense medium of air. Their thin bodies are easily torn and do not survive a rough initial deposit onto a beach. Like the cannonballs, however, they also eat plankton, and, as a result, their stings are not strong enough to be detected by us.

Not so for box jellies. These cubic, firm jellies have stout, tough tentacles on each lower corner of their two-inch-long bodies. Each of the four clusters of fingerlike tentacles trails longer, more delicate strands. They eat fish, and their sting is strong enough to kill a human under some circumstances. These glass-clear, nearly invisible boxes of venom close beaches in Australia to swimming when they arrive in the surf, for the Australian versions are larger and consequently deadly to people as well as to fish.

Because *Velella* is a sailboat, our passage is quiet and slow enough to watch marsh animals, including many kinds of birds. Each day we look forward to seeing birds that we have come to expect as escorts. We enter their world, often under their conditions, and they fly beside our sails as we slip along the marsh creeks. Our wake is rarely enough to disturb them.

This morning, as we depart the pleasant anchorage, it is low tide. Along muddy riverbanks, great blue herons and white great egrets stand poised perfectly still in the shallows, then lash out with their serpentine necks to strike at struggling silvery fish. Smaller snowy egrets and green herons are also lightning-fast and as common as the larger birds. In addition to marshes, we've seen them in marinas, where they prefer to fish, like trapeze artists, balanced on docking lines suspended over the water. They seem to unfurl to twice their length as they spear fish, without ever releasing the iron grip they maintain on the lines.

Happily, the numbers of these elegant wading birds have increased from severe historic lows, when they were decimated from hunting. The Audubon Society, its mascot a white egret, was founded in response to their plummet. The birds were killed for their pretty feathers, used to decorate women's hats. Their most striking feathers, long and comely, are only present during the breeding season, so birds in breeding plumage—the very animals who could reproduce the harvest—were killed, usually while nesting. Although it may astonish us that birds were killed solely for long plume feathers when fashion no longer dictates that women wear decorated hats, we can now buy snakeskin cowboy boots, mink fur coats, or kangaroo leather gloves. Or we can decorate our homes with shell-filled lamps, dried sea stars, shellacked puffer fish, and pieces of coral. All of them are dead animals. Only some of them are harvested sustainably so that we will have as many living animals in the future as we do in the present.

Somewhere along twisting channels in coastal Georgia, we see a new bird, one that neither of us has ever seen before. It is obviously an ibis because of its strongly decurved bill, but it is completely dark instead of white. "What in the world is that bird?" I ask and point it out to Ed.

"That's something new!" he exclaims. "Get the binoculars!" Ed slows us down so that we'll have longer to look. "Can you get it, Jennifer?"

I am confident it is not a juvenile white ibis, because although the young are brown, they usually travel with adults, and we are familiar with them. This bird is alone, and its plumage is a brilliant, reflective black with just a hint of dark green and russet. I get out the bird field guide to study while Ed has another look through the binoculars.

"Glossy ibis!" I proudly call after a few moments of flipping through the pages of the book. Ed makes a big circle in the river so that we can have another look. "Hey, thanks!" I say to him. "How did you know I hadn't seen enough of that bird?"

"I could see it in your face," he tells me.

I'd never seen a glossy ibis before, but there, in some unnamed quarter of marsh, the bird stands upon a muddy bank on the afternoon we sail by.

Before we cover another mile of river, a large flock of white ibis flies overhead. Their black wingtips on an otherwise white body cause their wings to appear short and square as they pass directly overhead. They land somewhere up ahead of us, and when we catch up to them, we see them feeding along the shoreline, probing shallow mudbanks with their pink, scimitar-shaped bills to jerk fiddler crabs from their burrows. Ed slows down again so that we can watch them feed, and I take over steering as I pass him the binoculars.

Before Hurricane Hugo hit the coast of South Carolina in 1989, Pumpkinseed Island in Winyah Bay supported a nesting colony of more than ten thousand of the birds, but the following year not a single white ibis nested there. Now, the largest nesting colony of white ibis along the east coast is on Battery Island in the Cape Fear River in North Carolina, where upward of twenty-six thousand birds nest. Other notable nesting sites occur in Texas, Louisiana, Florida, and elsewhere in the Carolinas, but the colonies move around and overall numbers are stable.

As we sail along rivers through coastal Georgia, we notice a subtle shift in the shape of the sounds. The rivers are more numerous, the currents less strong, and the sounds are smaller and better protected than those of South Carolina. These rivers, located south of the Savannah, arise in the coastal plain and thus have less force in their flow. Instead of ripping through an outlet to the sea, they meander behind sea islands, forming deltas with islands that arise and wash away as the river mouth migrates to open anew. I find I am much more comfortable because we rarely approach the opening to the sea where the currents and waves are more intimidating.

Like me, terns also seem more comfortable with the surroundings. In these protected waters, which are neither tiny, shallow creeks nor huge, open sounds, we see many more of them. The well-named least terns hover like butterflies in front of the bow before plunging headfirst into the water. Much larger Caspian and royal terns, with black crowns of feathers, dart in like arrows shot from a bow, then rise up again without ever ceasing to flap their wings.

All of these terns are clothed in gray and white feathers, and all fly with a deceptive leisureliness, innocently peering down into the water. When they see a fish, however, they suddenly fold their wings and plunge at amazing speed. Time and again, the birds unfurl their wings and pull out of the dive the instant before they hit, and I rock back on my heels with a gasp as they suddenly reverse their course. Medium-sized, gull-billed terns with thick, black bills sit on the pilings that outline the river's course as it passes under bridges. They, too, watch the water below them, then launch themselves as if from a diving platform to hurtle down in perfect form.

On this lucky afternoon, we are visited not only by terns, but by their relatives the skimmers. Skimmers are shaped much like terns, with very narrow, pointed wings, but are strikingly black above and white below, with very large, orange bills. Unconcerned by our presence, they pass silently by within arm's length of Velella's hull.

Both skimmers and terns fly low over the surface and open their bills so that the lower mandible pierces the water. The terns glide for only a few moments like this, and appear to skim the surface to drink a little water (albeit salty). The skimmers, however, maintain this posture while flying, with their elongated and knife-edged lower mandible deeply penetrating the water to catch small fish and shrimp. The tip of the orange mandible is black; the darker color must be less visible to potential meals than an orange tip would be. I stand on the bowsprit while they fly alongside us and look back to catch Ed watching me instead of the birds.

A few skimmers settle down to rest on a nearby sandbank. They are ungainly and comical with their very short legs, long wings, tuxedo-patterned coloration, and overly large, orange bills. They have an impressive underbite because the lower mandible is so much longer than the upper. We spin slowly around for another look, and our redirection startles them, but when they lift off and take to air, they are transformed into elegant and breathtakingly beautiful fliers. They so precisely follow the contours of the waves along the river's edge with so little apparent effort that they almost seem to be connected to water instead of to air.

Up ahead, a loud and distinctive call "Chee-*cheety*-chee, chee-*cheety*-chee" is shrieked by a different group of black-and-white birds. They wheel about over an oyster bank and land to feed, immediately revealing themselves as oystercatchers. They are shaped quite differently from the terns and skimmers, with longer legs, shorter wings, and bulkier bodies. Their bills are a bright red, redder even than skimmer's orange bills, but almost equally large.

Oystercatchers use their stout bills to open oysters by quickly slipping their bill into the slightly open gape, cutting the muscle that holds the two valves of the shell together, then extracting the oyster. There is some risk involved, for if the bird moves too slowly to cut the muscle before the valves close, the oystercatcher may be caught by the oyster instead, and drowned by a flooding tide. Only once have I actually seen a bird caught by an oyster, and it was a willet whose toe was stuck in a shell, or, perhaps, caught in fishing line that was wrapped around the shell. In either case, the bird freed itself before long.

While we watch the efficient feeders moving rapidly among the oysters, I remind Ed of the evening we ate a meal of nothing but roasted oysters, and he laughingly replies that he would like to see me try it with only a knife held in my mouth, mimicking the bill of birds. In addition to eating oysters, the birds also catch smaller and less well-protected animals that are associated with the mass of shell. Sometimes we open an oyster to find a pea crab living inside, and I think of those birds when I pop the little crab into my own mouth.

Sandpipers collect on nearly any sandy bank or shell mound in the marsh. In one narrow channel, a flock of small sandpipers flew across our bow with their white stomachs facing us, and then, turning, disappeared as effectively as a magician's trick when their darkly colored backs merged completely with the background of the water. They reappeared as the flock arose, dark backs highlighted against lighter sky. Like a school of fish or a perfectly synchronized orchestra, they acted in complete concert, turning in harmony and rising in a crescendo as a single unit instead of a group of distinct individuals. They found safety in their close choreography; when an individual became distinct from the flock it also became vulnerable.

It is a lone coot, a small, black, duck-like bird with a distinctive white bill, that a bald eagle plucks from the surface of the river. While steering, I see a coot that is separated from the rest of the flock, bobbing up away from them after one of its dives. When it pops up at some distance from the other coots, hardly a second passes before an eagle splits the sky overhead with its huge, dark body, snags the small coot in its yellow talons, and then leaps back toward the sky in moves so fast that the motion blurs. Alerted by my call, Ed shoots up out of the companionway to see the eagle already perched on a dead limb near its huge nest of sticks in a tall, dead pine, plucking feathers from the body of its prey before devouring the flesh.

By afternoon, it is hot, and we drop anchor in the middle of a wide river and swim in the coolness of the flowing current until the heat leaves us. We linger there, cooling off, until we are ready to move on. Back on deck, we motor only another mile before we find a satisfying creek anchorage, out of the way of traffic, with fifteen feet of water under our keel and a tidal range of less than six feet.

After coming to rest, we open the hatches wide and let the first evening breeze blow through the cabin. Within minutes, we return

Stingrays really do have stings. A spine on their tail is covered with venomous mucus that stings like that of a twenty-pound hornet if it breaks the skin of a handler. Although I've never been stung, I was once on a boat when a stingray came in fouled in a trawl net. The skipper was barely brushed by the sting, but it was painful enough that this big, burly man broke into a cold sweat and dropped to his knees on deck. The best treatment for a sting is to heat the area because the venom is a protein and damaged by heat. The boat crew had a heat pack in their first-aid kit and applied it to his wound; when we got back to shore, we also heated up water to as hot as his skin could stand and he immersed his swollen hand into it.

Skates, which are similar to rays, also occur in southeastern waters, but there is only one common species. Clear-nosed skates are so named because on either side of the skate's "nose" there are two clear patches of skin. Instead of a skinny tail on a big disk, their thick and short tail merges gradually into a wide body, and the whole body and tail is rougher and bumpier that the smooth skin of a ray. Skates look a little more believably like flattened sharks, and both skates and rays are more closely related to sharks than to bony fishes.

Skates lay eggs in tough, protective cases that the mother skate attaches to seagrasses or other objects that protrude above the muddy seafloor of the estuaries. As a child, I picked up the empty, black mermaid's purses that washed ashore and opened each one to look for a tiny skate inside, but never saw one. But once, while visiting a coastal aquarium, I saw golden cases that held living skate embryos, lighted from behind so that visitors could see the little skate with its yolk attached, as its heart beat and muscles twitched. Though skates lay eggs, rays give birth to their young, which swim away from their mother shortly after they are born.

The mouths of both skates and rays are on their undersides. The animals glide over the seafloor and suck up other creatures living there. In places where they have been feeding heavily, low tide reveals shallow depressions in the mud where they have stirred up the sediment and eaten the buried animals. Their gills open up on the underside, too, but these gill openings expel water and probably assist in feeding by blowing away some of the sediment. One pair of gills, the spiracles, opens on top of the head just behind the eyes, and the spiracles suck in clean water from above so that the fish can breathe.

After finishing our delicious supper, we stretch out on deck with our wineglasses to enjoy the evening. We sit quietly, happy to be in each other's company and with nothing much that needs to be said aloud. We are rewarded for our quiet vigilance as a school of dolphins surrounds us. We hear them breathing, with a quick and violent exhalation followed by an equally quick, but quieter, inhalation. That sound, of a hurried breath gasped in at the water's surface, is a powerful reminder of our kinship. I wonder if they ever miscalculate their quotient of air, and swim desperately for the surface, as I have done after swimming a little deeper than I thought. What happens if a wave breaks over their blowhole, as it has over my snorkel tube— do they come up sputtering and coughing until their lungs are clear? I wonder, too, if they dream of drowning, unable to reach the essential surface. But maybe they don't worry about the future, living instead fully in the present.

Dolphins sleep differently from the way we do. Instead of falling completely asleep, only one hemisphere of their brain rests at a time. Dolphins can swim and process information by using half their brain. Some large whales such as sperm whales sleep more like we do, resting on the surface with their blowholes well above water. Especially after a very deep dive, they may rest for hours. Whalers sometimes came upon these sleeping giants to make an easy kill.

Lulled by the dolphins' continual motion, I lean over onto Ed's chest. His hand touches my cheek, gently, and I look up into his face. Our lips meet, and, instantly, fish erupt from the water! We are startled back into awareness, confused by the reaction. Again, hunting dolphins charge the school of fish, scattering them into every direction including straight up. We hear dozens of reports as individual fish slam into the hull in a frenzied effort to escape. Some must stun themselves and make an easy meal for the dolphins.

The spell broken, I remind Ed of another afternoon, when we saw a school of mullet escape from dolphins by using *Velella*'s hull as a blind. They hung within centimeters of the hull, almost touching each other, while dolphins hunted nearby, and seemed to bubble out a fishy sigh of relief when the dolphins departed without ever detecting them. On that afternoon the dolphins went hungry.

Dolphins rely on their hearing, rather than their sight, to navigate murky waters. They produce high-pitched sounds that they focus into a sonar beam. When the sounds emitted by dolphins (and other whales) bounce off objects and return to them, the animals can detect the location of their food, each other, and even panes of glass that are invisible to human divers. Sperm whales, a close relative of dolphins, have a huge forehead full of oil to focus their sonar beam. It has even been suggested that they stun their prey of large squids with this focused beam of sound.

"Do you remember the dolphins we saw yesterday?" I ask. A group played in our bow wave as we sailed serenely. New mothers brought their tiny young ones to frolic beside us. The little ones were pink and small next to the large gray adults, but they kept up, born to swim and to surface.

"Of course!" he says, grinning, "How could I forget? You laughed yourself silly trying to point them out to me. 'Watch right there,' you'd say, and they'd come up behind us on the opposite side of the boat!"

Leaning over our lifelines, I had tried to predict where they would next arise, but they always fooled me, sometimes ahead, sometimes farther back, sometimes on our port side instead of starboard. I could never distinguish their surprisingly large, glistening gray backs until they were within inches of the surface. Breaking through, they caught a hurried breath and disappeared again into the tea-stained depths. I wondered, as I strained to see them, if they, too, were trying to catch a glimpse of me.

That night we sleep with the river gurgling pleasantly past us and dream fishy dreams. We awaken early the next morning in time to watch a glorious sunrise over the glasslike marsh creek. It is flat calm. Not even a ripple disturbs its reflective surface, in which the crescent moon is clearly visible. A marsh wren calls melodiously nearby, hidden in the marsh grass but with an unmistakable voice full of complex and bright-toned warbling. Now that it is low tide, a strip of dark mud separates the marsh grass from the river's edge.

A group of dolphins, probably the same acrobats of last night, churn the water just ahead into a boil. Slapping the surface with their tails, their bodies darting quickly above and below the surface, they are a maelstrom of motion. Suddenly fish and dolphins burst onto the mudbank, the dolphins quickly snatching a fish and then pulling themselves back into the water with efforts of their powerful tails. The dolphins make quite a breakfast of stranded mullet, although many fish manage to flip themselves back into the river. Our vision of the anchorage as a quiet, peaceful one surely differs from that of the other inhabitants of the creek.

These southeastern dolphins learned this trick of herding fish onto mudbanks and taught each other the method, for they are the only population of bottlenose dolphins who perform this feat. A continent away, on the east coast of South America, killer whales have learned a similar method. Here they charge ashore to grab unwary seals from steep beaches. As far as we know, these are the only two places on Earth where marine mammals chase their prey on land, a dim remembrance of their evolutionary past.

We raise anchor and head farther south, in rivers that look like rivers only at low tide. As the tide rises, the river stretches out its fingers and then its arms into the marshes until we look for miles and miles at an immense expanse of silvery-black water and green marsh grass. For a while, trees are barely visible on each horizon, where the mainland or outer barrier island provides a foothold for them, but they are so distant as to appear only as slightly darker blurs of vegetation. Eventually, however, we begin to see a few islands scattered in the marsh.

On those islands with some permanent land, marked by live oaks, palmettos, myrtles, and an occasional pine, a few hardy souls have settled. Their houses are scarcely visible, surrounded by the greenery, but a spindly pier extending out to the river identifies the human habitation. The secluded houses usually have large cisterns to store rainwater, and a boat at the end of the dock with which to commute to the mainland or a larger island for supplies. The houses and piers cling tenuously to the emergent land, as though the river could just shrug its shoulders or make one swipe with its dripping hand and easily be free of the pesky intruder.

As we pass a simple but elegant house on a beautiful and isolated small island, we see a woman leave her rocking chair and come to her doorway. From behind her screen door she silently raises her hand in greeting as we slowly enter, then exit, her world. That gently raised hand seems to be a signal of recognition that we, like she, have experienced the reality of nature by escaping for a while from the illusions of society; that we have seen and heard and become part of the salt marsh. I wonder if she remembers us, as her memory haunts my own recollection of those Georgia islands.

St. Simons Island to
St. Marys Entrance

AFTER SEVERAL WEEKS OF ADVENTURE ON OUR OWN, OUR confidence has grown, but our skills are still in their infancy. We pull into a nice marina on St. Simons Island and decide to phone a couple of friends to join us for the weekend. Our friends are biologists, too, and have been hearing the stories of our new boat and fantastic collecting trips. They even came down one cold March weekend to stay aboard while we worked on improvements and repairs to *Velella*. We feel as though we owe them a good time after all the work they've put in, and we want to show off.

Because we have already discussed this portion of the cruise with them, they are ready to shove off as soon as they get our call. We dock at a marina by noon, and they are aboard by evening. Since it is Friday night, the local restaurant is hopping with live music, crowded tables, good food, and plenty of libations. We consider it a great sendoff for our adventure together.

Early the next morning, boat motors start revving up before dawn. The big offshore fishing boat tied up next to us is going out to fish for the day, based on all the loud conversation and their endless trips rolling gear past us. We are soon up and awake, the four of us maneuvering past each other between the head, galley, and berths, stowing away sleeping gear, preparing breakfast, listening to weather reports, and discussing the upcoming day.

The forecast is for beautiful weather, winds from the north, pleasantly cool, and an absence of the typical afternoon thunderstorms. As we tidy up, our excitement grows in anticipation of adventure: an offshore cruise south from St. Simons Sound to St. Marys Entrance. Both inlets are well-marked, deep channels and only about twenty miles apart, so that we can easily make it back in before dark. We plan to sail offshore all day Saturday, anchor somewhere along the ICW Saturday night, then motor up the ICW on Sunday, arriving back at the marina in plenty of time for our friends to drive home Sunday night and return to their jobs on Monday morning. But before me lies not one, but two of those inlets I dislike.

We depart the marina and raise the sails within minutes. Before we are even halfway out of the inlet, however, the new automatic bilge pump Dan left us quits working, and the bilge begins to fill with water. With light morning air, we make little headway under sail on the incoming tide, and bob like a cork in the rough inlet waters rather than slicing through the sea.

In hindsight, we should have doused the sails, cranked up the motor, and turned around right then. We didn't. In a poor decision born of inexperience, we decide instead to repair the bilge pump while sailing through the confused sea. Ed adjusts the pump and gets it working again, but he turns a sickly color of green from hanging nearly upside down in the smelly bilge while we roll and pitch through the rough inlet. It doesn't help that the bilge water is contaminated with an oily stench of diesel fuel.

With Ed now more or less out of commission from seasickness, all the steering, navigation, and decision making falls to me. Of the four of us, only Ed and I have done any amount of sailing, and limited at that. One of our two guests has never set foot on a sailboat other than *Velella*.

The offshore waters are rough, and the inlet channel seems to go on forever. Finally we pass the last buoy and turn south. With a little wind behind us and free of the current in the channel, *Velella* steadies herself and we begin to make some headway. Ed changes from green back to a more normal color, but is still unsteady, so I keep the helm.

When we sight the buoys marking St. Marys Entrance a few hours later, we all breathe a sigh of relief. However, the channel is positioned so that we actually have to sail south of it, then make the turn inland to start the run. The wind is now nearly directly ahead, and after two uncomfortable tacks from one channel marker to the other, I begin to rethink the whole idea of coming in under sail. The closer to land we approach, the less wind we have as the land blocks it, and by now the tide has turned and is roaring out of the channel. Once again, we are traversing an inlet with the tide against us, and once again rough waters make everyone a little queasy. It is my call to douse the sails, but we've all had enough of sailing anyway, and no one complains when I crank up the diesel to give us some power against the current.

Ed has recovered enough to steer while I lower sails. I disconnect the jib halyard, the rope that raises and lowers the sail, to keep it from sliding up and down the mast with each passing wave while under motor power. Through a stroke of bad luck, we hit a wave at a critical moment, and the halyard-to-sail connector jumps open from its temporary attachment where I'd clipped it at the base of the mast. Since the rope end of the halyard is longer and heavier than the wire end with the connector on it, the end with the connector immediately shoots to the top of the mast while the other end descends like an Arabian rope when the charmer's music stops. Its descent finally ends when the connector itself smashes into the roller of the mast-top and lodges there. I spend a few moments standing on deck, feeling foolish about allowing the halyard to jump free, but then begin to coil up the long end of the halyard while reflecting on how we will fix the problem. Finally, I realize what we must do. We won't take the mast down or even hire a crane. We will use the mainsail halyard to pull someone to the top of the mast and retrieve the connector end of the jib halyard. Thank goodness we hadn't lost them both!

Once inshore in calmer waters, we pore over charts to find an anchorage. We consider docking at a pier on Cumberland Island, but since we still have a few hours of daylight, we decide to go farther north. We also want to be out of the way of any nuclear subs coming or going from the nearby Kings Island base. Once while sailing in Charleston Harbor, we were nearly swamped by the enormous wake of a nuclear sub. Their scale is beyond imagination; men on the conning tower look like ants, and their wake isn't noticeable until the sub is gone and a fifteen-foot wave is crashing down on your bow. We find a nice anchorage and set the hook with the sun still in the sky.

With Ed recovered by now from the inlet, his curiosity gets the best of him. Where is all that water in the bilge coming from? The bilge pump is still running almost constantly. As soon as it quits, the bilge rapidly fills with water, which is not a comforting situation. Ed crawls into the hot engine room as soon as we are anchored securely. Within a few minutes, he discovers that the stuffing box, the collar sealing the propeller shaft as it passes through the hull, is leaking terrifically. The box is designed to cool the shaft as water drips through it, but gallons are pouring through ours. We understand the concept, but have no experience with how much water is really supposed to come through—one little drip hardly seems like enough to cool the turning propeller shaft, but gallons seem unnecessary. What is enough?

I read instructions to Ed from our book on engine maintenance and suggest that he just needs to make a few "simple" adjustments to the stuffing box in order to tighten it down. I am sitting on deck, a cool breeze on my face and an ice-cold drink in my hands, chatting amiably with our guests, while Ed is in the hot, stinking engine room smashing his knuckles against the greasy propeller shaft as he tries to tighten the nuts on the stuffing box. When I ask for a second time what is taking him so long and then complain that he is making us wait for supper, he bursts from the engine room hatch, hot and frustrated by the frozen nuts and angered by my unsympathetic comments. I think his anger is misdirected; he thinks my snippy comments are uncalled for; but we are both too stubborn to make amends.

Luckily, Ed is so sweaty and uncomfortable that he leaps overboard for a swim, still clad in his dirty shirt and shorts, overheated and greasy from bumping around in the tiny, stifling engine room. As he sighs in relief and pleasure from the cool water, our two guests decide to put on their swimsuits and follow him. After stubbornly watching them for a few minutes as they enjoy the water, I finally give up and join them. The river's cool current puts everyone in a different frame of mind and erases the stresses of the day. I manage a supper of light fare, and we all feel a little better.

We learned more about stuffing boxes a couple of months later, after hauling-out for a bottom job of paint and repair. On opening up the stuffing box, we found that there was essentially no flax packing left in the box, which is the key item that prevents seawater from rushing into the boat from the gap around the propeller shaft; as we wallowed through the rough inlet water, the wiggling shaft dislodged the little bit of worn-out flax. Ed couldn't tighten down the nuts because there were no turns left on the bolt. No wonder he'd kept smashing his knuckles as he attempted to tighten down a nut on nonexistent threads!

During the next morning, rested and recovered from the previous day's adventures, we tackle the problem of retrieving the halyard. Impatient to be on the move, we raise anchor as soon as everyone is awake and motor along the secluded, narrow waterway. With Ed harnessed into the bosun's chair, I winch him aloft, cranking the main winch for all I am worth. One of our companions steers and the other stands by to tail lines and assist me as needed. We raise Ed in the chair as if raising a sail, though I must pause on several occasions to rest my arms and back. Everything goes rather smoothly until we near a sharp bend in the channel.

Perched at the mast-top, well over fifty feet above the water, Ed can see what is blocked from our view by tall marsh grass: a tugboat pushing a long, loaded barge is steaming on a course to intersect with us precisely at the sharp bend and will need nearly the entire river to negotiate it. Ed shouts down instructions from above while we make a few tight circles, hoping we remain within the deeper confines of the narrow channel and nervous about grounding in the shallows while the barge approaches. Finally, the huge vessel pushes by us. Its wake, thankfully, is minimal and only slams Ed once against the mast. As he descends with the wayward halyard and sore knees, I vow to "ride the chair" if I ever make the same mistake again. I do.

But our mistakes on this trip aren't over yet. We leave our friends steering and navigating while Ed and I clean up the gear from his trip up the mast. Since they are enjoying themselves, I even try a few casts with my fishing rod, but we are moving too quickly for me to reel the lure back in correctly. Unable to find anything else to do, I go below to stow the bosun's chair back in the farthest corner of the boat, but have trouble and call Ed down to help. Suddenly there is a terrible noise and both Ed and I pitch forward onto the floor. We leap up, run up the gangway, and find our two friends arguing over the chart. Ed shouts to cut the motor because we are still in forward, but we aren't moving. We have grounded hard. Ed tries everything, from reverse at full throttle to alternating between forward and reverse, to turning the rudder hard while in forward. Nothing works and the tide is falling. We know we are stuck for a long while, because we must wait for low water, which is still four hours away, which means four more until the tide is back to this height, then another one or two hours until we float off: we figure nine hours at a minimum.

We sit at a crazy angle on a mudbank for the rest of the day. The tides of the Southeast have such a wide range—eight feet is common—that we actually come entirely out of the water for a short time and could walk completely around the boat if we want to. No one wants to.

The hours pass slowly. There is no way we will make it back to the marina today, which means that our friends are going to miss a day of work. But it was our friends who were steering and navigating and who put us on the mudbank. Even though it is early, we have supper, barely sustain a conversation, and call it an evening as soon as we can. Ed and I go below to bed.

Being beginners, it doesn't occur to us to put out an anchor when we are stuck firmly aground, but sure enough, the tide eventually floods beyond our grounding point and we float free. I awake to a panicked shout from one of our guests, who is luckily still awake and up on deck. He has suddenly realized that a strong current is pulling us rapidly toward a nearby bridge. He probably saved *Velella* from destruction; if it had been just Ed and me, we'd have hit the bridge before we knew we were floating.

We scramble about on deck, tripping over all manner of items and still dazed from the panicked awakening, trying to locate channel markers and figure out where we are, all in total darkness except for the sinisterly illuminated bridge. Somehow we locate the key, get the engine started, and motor away from the bridge until we find deep enough water to set the anchor for the rest of the night. We suspect that we are dead center of the channel, not out of it, and hope that another barge doesn't ply the river during the night. I doubt that I am the only one who awakens every hour and peers out the portholes, looking for the lights of an approaching barge.

We are up before dawn the next day, everyone ready to get somewhere else, but it is not to be. When Ed reaches for the engine and turns the key, all we hear is a click. Just "click-click-click" as he desperately tries to start it. Hearing the unfamiliar sound, I immediately poke my head up the companionway to see what is happening. Ed is cursing under his breath and trying again and again, to no avail. I go back down below since there is nothing I can do. When our guests pick up on the problem, I can nearly feel steam rising from them. Another day stuck in the marsh; we are now two full days off schedule. Ed works hard all day on the problem. I try to lend him my support without getting in his way, and stay near the small opening into the engine room so that I can provide him with whatever he needs. I finally hear a wonderful sound: the engine cranks.

I am amazed by his ability to diagnose the engine problem with only a few good books to help him. He worked all day on it, constantly referring to his books. He tested possibility after possibility until he discovered where the problem lay. He created an ingenious solution as repair. When that engine finally cranks, my husband positively gleams from among the beads of sweat and black streaks of engine grease on his forehead. Those few hours reveal much of his personality to me.

"Your mother would be so proud!" I say. "And your wife is both proud and grateful!"

"Well, your navigation at sea put us right on top of those sea buoys!" he says to me, smiling through the grease. "I'll keep making the repairs if you keep telling me the route."

"We seem to be on course."

We motor for a few hours and are able to reach the marina just as it is getting dark. We eat a simple dinner while motoring so that our guests can unload and drive home as soon as we hit the dock. While we are sitting on deck, looking toward the now visible marina, one of our guests asks why Ed didn't just call a repairman instead of doing all that hard work on his own. After all, we weren't very far from the marina, and a repairman in a fast powerboat could have made it to us in an hour. Ed pauses, his eyes boring into her, and answers, "First, because it's my boat. If you are going to own a boat, you ought to be able to make repairs. Second, because we could have been sailing somewhere other than along the coast of Georgia, where there might not be a handy repairman. If I want to be able to fix my boat in Sri Lanka, then I might as well begin learning in Georgia. Third, the option to call a repairman has always been available to me today.

If I'd been unable to make the repair, I would have called. Sailing is more than just an afternoon trip. It's a commitment to a lifestyle."

After our friends leave, Ed and I try to figure out what went wrong as we clean up and reestablish the interior to our liking. Perhaps it wasn't too surprising that so much stress and unhappiness developed. We experienced a stuffing-box leak, bilge-pump failure, halyard difficulties, running aground, and engine trouble. Each one of these setbacks delayed us and was seen as a problem instead of an opportunity to learn. We were all separate individuals trying to get somewhere, and that focus on the destination instead of the trip meant that when we failed to reach our destination on time, the trip failed as well. That vision, too, of four friends going somewhere was hindered by the focus on four. In reality we were one group, dependent on each other, not four independent individuals, but our egos prevented us from seeing the truth of our interrelationship. Instead, we became annoyed with each other, blaming others for the problems. And we just left *Velella* out of the whole mix when she was the one supporting us. We forgot about anchoring her, we nearly let her hit a bridge, and we ran her aground, poor girl.

After this set of misadventures, things began to get easier. We laugh, and sometimes shudder, at all the things we did wrong at the beginning, but we learned a lot from our mistakes. A new boat might have made it easier on us, but old *Velella* taught us a lot and provided us with countless memories. We were rewarded with beautiful blue skies, cool crisp days, nights of steady offshore sailing and nights peacefully anchored in quiet creeks, but we also have memories of moments of excitement, even a few of fear, all of which combine into a patchwork quilt of recollections.

Our friend who introduced us to sailing once told us that sailing was 90 percent boredom and 10 percent terror. I would amend that to say that the first six months is nearly all in the terror category, while the rest of all the sailing years fall into the category of 90 percent peacefulness, interspersed with a few rushes of adrenaline. Those rushes nearly always come with a new experience, be it frightening or exhilarating. The only difference between the two seems to be mental evaluation of the action. How boring life would be without those opportunities, fraught with fear or excitement, that are the essence of learning.

Ed and I learn, too, about ourselves, discovering what links together the joys and frustrations of our experiences. When we allow ourselves to appreciate every part of the trip, we recognize each trip as an opportunity for discovery. Time begins to matter less; traveling begins to matter more. We both begin to see our egos as stumbling blocks to understanding. Our dreams start to become real as false perceptions of our everyday lives are revealed. We are at the beginning of a voyage of discovery. Is this a solid vessel for our dreams?

Florida

It hardly seems possible, but it is now five months since we bought *Velella* in February and more than a month into our first long cruise. Leaving our friends at the marina on St. Simons Island, we start south again, retracing our steps toward St. Marys Entrance, the inlet that separates Georgia from Florida.

Moving slowly along the ICW, we remember to rejoice in our slow progression. Measuring each day on the water as an interstate hour, we are freed from speed. We allow ourselves the time to watch the wildlife, enjoy the watery vistas, and to move into comfortable positions. All these seemingly simple pleasures are denied in the frenzied rush from point to point on I-95, the interstate that parallels our watery route. Friends and family worry constantly during our transit while afloat, but ignore the greater actual risks of travel by car. Somehow, the dangers posed by other people and their vehicles seem less threatening than the vagaries of nature that we might encounter on our watery route.

What these anxious relatives do not realize is that we are all part of that one vast entity of historical relationships and functional interdependencies known as nature. Instead, they seem to think that humanity exists outside nature, that a clean and sterile world will free us of our dependence on the natural world and our origin in it. Where they see imprisoning chains, we see silken threads that weave everything in nature, including us, into a vibrant, living fabric. Why is there such reluctance to face our own biological origins and behaviors? It is a fight of duality: humanity versus nature, but it is a fight we cannot win, because it does not exist. Humans are built of the same basic stuff as the jellies floating in the sea, and we are members of the same organic orchestra. Ed and I choose to swim counter to the usual current so that we can hear the song of the salt marsh.

I open my eyes to the first rays of sun and find Ed, also awake, looking at me. Neither of us needs an alarm clock any longer. When the sun rises, so do we. We putter around, checking the engine and sails, eating breakfast until the sun is far enough above water to start a breeze. Heavy dew on the decks begins to dry after some help from a sponge. A great blue heron stalks the riverbanks, searching for his breakfast, too. Neither of us is in a hurry to leave the idyllic anchorage. We have set aside our need to be elsewhere and are satisfied, instead, with where we are.

We are glad to be together again, just two of us aboard *Velella*. We notice how quiet it seems, how spacious *Velella* feels. We were so easily drawn back into the everyday world that our friends still inhabit, the world we are learning to escape and to question. The long weekend was stressful, too short to get into the flow of nature, and too many complications to make for an easy passage. Instead of helping them adjust to our new world, we returned to theirs, leaving us disappointed in our role as teachers. But we'll have other opportunities; after all, we are still students ourselves, learning to sail and learning to see.

Entering Florida, we return to a bustling world of humanity. The salt marshes, formerly so vast, narrow into a strip along each side of the waterway and eventually disappear. White sandy beaches adorn straighter channels. Instead of enormous empty sounds and strong river currents, there are shallow lagoons with fewer outlets to the sea. The banks along the ICW are crowded with houses, often just a stone's throw from the channel markers, and the waterway is filled with other boaters.

We approach St. Marys Entrance on an incoming tide. The water is azure blue and laps gently at a snowy-white strand, wavelets sparkling brilliantly in the sun. The desolate beauty of Cumberland Island, the southernmost island in Georgia, is accentuated by free horses that come down to the water's edge to forage, heads tossing and manes flying as they gallop along a sandy shore. The horses parallel our route until they reach the island's terminus, then they wheel back into the interior and gallop away. We never saw them, or least didn't notice them, when we passed this same island heading north with our friends. I guess we had others things on our minds.

Fort Clinch stands across the inlet on the Florida side, and although its visible structures date from the time of the Civil War, ruins of earlier Spanish and English fortifications abound in the area. The horses of Cumberland Island, descendants of stallions and mares left behind by the Spanish soldiers, and the ruins themselves are silent reminders of that earlier period in Florida's history. This coast, now settled and so ordered that even the ocean's tides are channeled past rock jetties, was wild and remote to those first Spanish soldiers who left behind their forts and their horses.

The Guale and Mocama were two tribes of Native Americans who lived along what is now the Georgia and north Florida coasts. The Spanish explorers who settled St. Augustine set up additional missions within their territories and tried to convert the Natives to Christianity. But the Westo, the same tribe of slave traders who harassed the Natives around the Charles Towne and Port Royal settlements, also enslaved members from these two tribes, and epidemic diseases introduced by the Europeans decimated them. By the time that Charles Towne was a decade old, the Guale and Mocama were extinct as distinct tribes, with the few survivors incorporated into the Yamasee.

After enjoying the wildness of Cumberland Island, the beauty of the deep and clear inlet, and the nostalgia of the old fort, a heavily industrialized commercial port just south of the inlet assaults all our senses. It is incredibly ugly and depressing to experience after traveling slowly through salt marshes. Gigantic steel structures reach into the sky. An incessant humming occasionally punctuated by startling clangs and screeches of metal on metal permeates the air as the machinery operates. My eyes water as we move through a plume of dark smoke that hangs directly in our path, and even the air feels heavy on my skin. This is progress? The juxtaposition of Cumberland Island with the port is too stark to leave any question of humanity's uncontrolled excesses and resultant defects, its drive to master rather than to harmonize with the natural world. Eventually, however, a bend in the river puts the port behind, and nature reasserts its beauty.

Even though humans have encroached on and altered the natural habitat, the water's edge is still a place that supports lives other than our own. Most of these lives we know little about, although they fascinate many among us, leading us to spend our lives trying to understand theirs, for to understand a part deeply is to comprehend the whole. As Rachel Carson concludes in *The Edge of the Sea*, "Contemplating the teeming life of the shore, we have an uneasy sense of the communication of some universal truth that lies just beyond our grasp." This transitional area, between the sea that we have not conquered, and the land that we have claimed for ourselves, has its secrets that we have yet to learn. Whether bird or fish or oyster reef, spartina or algae or great live oak, all rely on the edge of the sea, as Rachel Carson recognized, beginning her book with the sentence, "The edge of the sea is a strange and beautiful place." Here is where the rhythm of the tides is the only clock that matters, where ghost crabs wait for the sea's caress so that they might release their young into its care, then return to their burrows above the mark of high water.

As soon as we turn again into the purity of marsh, just south of the port, we are greeted by a flock of white pelicans. White pelicans occur more often on the gulf coast of Florida, but this flock has made the east coast near Fernandina Beach its permanent home; we saw them on subsequent trips as well. They are spectacular birds, with wingspans of nine feet, larger even than the more familiar brown pelicans. They have a sort of majesty about them, as do the browns, and fly steadily along like elegant old gentlemen. The white feathers, like pure white hair, enhance their stateliness. As we watch a group floating with us in the waterway, a second flock flies overhead. The pelican leading the V-formation drops back to rest and another takes its place, cutting a swath for others to follow.

While excitedly watching white pelicans and trying to capture their images, I am surprised to see a bald eagle standing regally on one of the mounds of pearly oyster shell that flank the channel. We sail within a few yards of the bird, and it watches us warily through brilliant golden eyes. To approach it so closely allows us to truly gauge its impressive size, standing three feet tall, its sharply hooked beak as lethal as the curved blade of a steel carpet knife and its feet and toes as large as my own hand and fingers. It does not appear intimidated by our close approach, never even shrugging its feathers to indicate annoyance. It merely stands on its palatial mound of shell and surveys its domain, the sharp talons of one enormous yellow foot piercing the body of a mullet, its next meal.

I wonder if it is the same bird when, a day or so later, we sit aground in the very center of the marked channel around Matanzas Inlet. We are confused at our inability to maneuver through shoals. With a sense of inevitability, we watch as a tugboat pushing a loaded barge reading nine feet of draft approaches us. Before it is even near us, however, it turns out of the marked channel and passes by us a hundred feet or more away. The current refuses to flow in its designated channel, and we have been trapped into believing that the markers determine where the channel lies, instead of the other way around.

"Well, damn!" I say, watching the tug as it negotiates the channel. "We are dead center of the marked channel and that guy is not even close!"

"You'd think they'd move the buoys," Ed replies.

"So now we know where the channel is. What next?" I turn to Ed.

"We wait."

I lie back on the cabintop, absorbing warm sun through half-closed eyes, noticing the slightest breeze that tickles my cheek with a strand of hair. When an object passes between my body and the sun to cast a cool shadow on my skin, I open my eyes to see an eagle suspended in cloudless blue firmament, its dark, flat wings outspread, spiraling upward until it disappears into brightness. When I sit up, the bird is nowhere to be seen.

We have three hours until the tide turns and releases us from the bottom. The eagle turns my mind toward fish, and I head below to rescue my fishing pole from its stowage in the quarter-berth. It is already rigged with a trout-tout lure, and within minutes I am casting from the foredeck out toward the channel. In only a few casts, I hook a nice spotted sea trout, which is strong and large enough to fight several minutes. When Ed sees it, his interest peaks, and he sets aside the book he is reading and takes over the rod and reel while I clean the fish. By the time I finish cleaning, he has not felt a single strike and is ready to return to the book. On my very next cast, I have another trout! Ed raises his eyebrows at that and says that he must have been attracting the fish into the area for me. He takes the rod and tries again while I clean the second fish. When he still catches nothing, he turns the fishing completely over to me. Within another cast or two, fish number three is on my line, and this time, Ed volunteers to clean it so that I can continue to fish. I quit after landing the fourth fish, for that makes two evening meals and fills our small refrigerator. When the tide finally returns, we slowly edge into the channel and count our grounding as a fishing trip.

Later that same day we leave twisting channels for the vast shallowness of Mosquito Lagoon. Through the shimmering of afternoon heat we can just make out the huge Vehicle Assembly Building at the Kennedy Space Center. Arguably one of our most technologically advanced designs, the space shuttles were built here, among these extensive natural lagoons. The isolation afforded by the shallow marshes not only benefits the space program, but bird and manatee populations as well through the Merritt Island National Wildlife Refuge.

One of the most memorable birds we saw at the refuge during a winter visit was a marbled godwit. Built like a sandpiper on steroids, it has a rounded body, long legs, and a long bill, but its key character for identification is that its bill turns upward. I remember observing a flock of various shorebirds, all of them similar in shape and all in their brownish winter plumage. As I despaired of ever identifying them, I suddenly noticed the upturned bill of one bird and could name it as a godwit. By focusing on small details, I distinguished the bird from the throng.

An endless series of channel markers delineates the limits of our excursions in our deep-draft boat, but tiny johnboats gleefully crisscross the vast, flat lagoon. As night falls, we realize that we must anchor along the edge of the long, straight channel, but its edges are so sharp from the teeth of the dredge that I read four feet off the bowsprit, using our sounding line, while Ed keeps the stern in ten or twelve feet of water.

Standing on the bow pulpit, heaving the lead line out forward, then reading the depth from a series of knots in the line as the line becomes vertical, we hearken back to the days of old sailing ships, when the leadsman in the chains would continue to sound the depth during nearshore battles or excursions until the captain called him off. Described so well by C. S. Forester in his Horatio Hornblower novels, the leadsman assumed complete responsibility for a constant report of depth. Even if the captain ordered the ship back out to sea, and the leadsman began to read "no-bottom" on his line, he continued to call out until he received an order to halt, and could be flogged for ceasing his reports without a direct order to do so. The nearshore currents, especially the unpredictable swirls around inlets, can drop out shoals of sand in unexpected places and change from day to day.

There is nothing as satisfying as knowing the exact depth of a new anchorage or shoal area before the boat is upon it. With the lead line, I know the depth at the tip of the bowsprit instead of at the boat's midpoint, where our depth-sounder is located. I suppose someone sounding with a lead line must seem an anachronism, but I feel more comfortable knowing that the line is touching actual bottom. Too often, our depth-sounder is fooled by a false bottom, especially if sediment has been stirred up into the water. In fact, Ed had just switched off the depth-sounder after repeated frantic electronic warnings of an imminent grounding kept us on pins and needles while we moved through what was actually sufficient depth of water. The water was just so muddy through this stretch with all the busy boat traffic that the depth-sounder was fooled. Once we both realized how irritable we felt and recognized that the cause was the constant buzz of the depth-sounder, we cut it off and relaxed.

"Now, that's better!" I say to Ed from the bowsprit. "Every time I hear that beeping start, it makes me anxious."

"Me, too," Ed says. "You've got the right answer there in your hand. Remember this morning as we tried to find the actual channel around Matanzas? That guy on the big, fancy cruiser stared open-mouthed at you as we sounded through the shoal water with the lead line."

"Yeah," I chuckle, "he was trying to be so helpful by calling out the readings from his own depth-sounder, then promptly hit a sandbar as we edged right past them with our near six feet of draft. I hope they got free!"

After three attempts along different sections of the channel, we finally find a place that provides seven feet just outside the channel. Perhaps it is a natural depression in the shallow lagoon. Was it formed by a whale eons ago, when the sea was higher? Or by an extinct eastern bison more recently, only ten thousand years ago, when more of the sea was trapped in glacial ice and this lagoon was land instead?

"It could have been a wallow for any of the extinct North American megafauna," Ed suggests. "A ground sloth, or short-faced bear, or giant beaver. Any one of those or many others."

"Some great fossils have been discovered not too far from here. Those sloths were about ten feet tall! What do you suppose the first inhabitants of these lands thought about finding bones of giant animals? Maybe the very first Natives even got to see the living animals ten thousand years ago!"

Throughout the night, awakened by the whine of hungry mosquitoes on the other side of the hatch's netting, I get up to check our position, hoping that our stern has not swung out into the shallows or into the way of an oncoming barge. More than once, I awake to clinging dreams of mastodons, beavers the size of pigs, and tiny horses no bigger than collies all marching across the dry, fern-filled lagoon toward the towering Vehicle Assembly Building.

Early the next morning we are up and moving even before the sun has completely risen. Ahead is Haulover Canal, though which will we pass from Mosquito Lagoon into the Indian River Lagoon.

When Spaniards arrived in Florida in 1513, they encountered Ais and Timucuan tribes along this section of the coast. The first contact, in fact, was likely to have occurred right here, when Ponce de Leon landed near Cape Canaveral. The Ais undoubtedly encountered more Spanish explorers, and by the time that St. Augustine was founded in 1565, the Ais and Spanish were acquainted with each other.

In addition to diseases and horses, the Spanish also brought citrus to Florida. The first cultivated oranges were grown in this area in 1828 when a breeder used some of the naturalized, Floridian plants as his stock, outbreeding them with other varieties. William Bartram traveled through Florida as well as the Carolinas in the 1770s and wondered whether citrus trees were native, but the Spanish brought them, most likely two or nearly three centuries earlier, and the Native Americans recognized their value and cultivated the trees. Similarly, peaches were already present in South Carolina when John

Lawson arrived in 1700, and he thought that they might be native, but Spanish and Native American trade had long before established them in the region.

Emerging into Haulover Canal from Mosquito Lagoon, we forgot our long night as we delighted in magnificent birding. Throughout Mosquito Lagoon, Haulover Canal, and the Indian River, small islands, made up of dredge spoil, line the channel like beads on a necklace. Haulover Canal was first constructed in 1854, but enlarged by the Army Corps of Engineers in the 1930s as part of the ICW project. The birds have taken advantage of these human-formed islands, and a few of the islands are claimed by the birds as nesting rookeries or as overnight roosts.

Stately, white great egrets as well as snowy egrets, their smaller, yellow-footed cousins, rise up from their fishing grounds along the muddy banks, gracefully wing their way toward the islands, and settle into a few isolated trees until the trees seem to bloom with white-petaled flowers. When great egrets, snowy egrets, white ibises, and pelicans take to wing from among their roosting trees, they remind me of a speeded-up film clip of blooming magnolia flowers. In the shadows of nests of large pelicans or wading birds, smaller birds find protection for their nests. No eagle would risk the sword-like bills of the big birds, effectively protecting defenseless birds that build below their unsuspecting guardians.

Our favorite unusual Florida bird is undoubtedly the roseate spoonbill. We know to watch for them along Haulover Canal, for we've seen several during our land-based trips to Merritt Island National Wildlife Refuge. The farthest north we have ever seen one is at Fernandina Beach, although they reportedly occur as far north as South Carolina as occasional summertime visitors. Spoonbills are bright pink, large birds, and could be mistaken for flamingos except for their bill. Instead of the down-curved, banana-shaped bill of flamingos, spoonbills have bills that widen at the tip into a shallow spoon.

Both flamingos and spoonbills have specialized feeding habitats, as might be guessed from the unusual shapes of their bills. Both use their bills to catch the small crustaceans that live in the sediment; spoonbills by moving the two mandibles back and forth, and flamingos by straining the water through their bill. They are dependent on the animals they eat for their beautiful color, and if kept in captivity, must be fed a special diet that contains some of their natural food or their colors will fade away. They spend much of their time feeding with their heads lowered, sometimes even underwater, and this habit makes them vulnerable and unable to see approaching danger. A few sentry birds always stand guard as the flock feeds, and when one sentry leaves its post in order to feed, another bird takes its place. Because of this behavior, it is impossible to approach a bird unawares unless it is alone.

Once we pass from Haulover Canal to the Indian River, brown pelicans are common. In 1970, they were federally listed as an endangered species, but their numbers have increased since the phase-out of DDT, and in 2009 they were delisted as a species (the East Coast population including Florida was delisted in 1985). Bald eagles were delisted in 2007 for similar reasons; they had been listed as endangered in 1967. These birds symbolize the success we can achieve if we listen to people like Rachel Carson, take the appropriate steps, and do the right thing.

The birds seem to be quite a distance from their rookeries, but then I realize that the distance from their rookeries on the dredge-spoil islands to their feeding grounds on the Indian River was not as far for them to fly as it was for us to sail the angled channel. I had always assumed that pelicans fed on large fish, which they caught in the pouch formed by their throat and bill after diving headlong into the water. Although large fish may compose part of their food, they also feed on schools of very small fish. As John Malcolm Brinnin describes, "All of a sudden came the pelicans:/crazy old men in baseball caps, who flew/like jackknives and collapsed like fans."

Flying low over the water, a pelican passes us on the port side, then suddenly collapses into a shallow dive while swinging its net-like bill from one side to the other in the water. It makes the same motion with its bill that a human with a long-handled dip net would make if trying to collect and concentrate a school of minnows in the net. With an absurdly satisfied look on its face, the pelican, now floating quietly, stretches up its head and neck to swallow, flipping back a few small fry hanging from the corners of its mouth.

The local gulls also notice the protruding fish. The pelican has just made a second successful dive and now has a ring-billed gull floating next to it. This time, the pelican keeps his head underwater until the last possible moment, then quickly raises his head to swallow the fish as the gull attempts to steal the pelican's catch by grabbing the dangling minnows from its mouth.

"Are you watching this?" Ed asks me.

"Sure am!" I reply. "Look—there's another one! That gull is following the pelican like a baby brother!" This time, after the pelican surfaces from its dive, the gull actually lands on its back and tries to grab some of the fish from its mouth.

"Can you believe this?" Ed asks. "There's another pair way over there! What's going on here?" Assuming we had observed a new interaction between species, we record our observations in a notebook we keep on board. Sometime later, while reading *Book of Bays* by William Beebe, the deep-sea explorer, ichthyologist, ornithologist, and prolific author of captivating natural-history books, I read his identical observations of laughing gull–brown pelican interactions along Mexico's west coast in the Rio Dulce near Acapulco. We observed the bird interactions along the northern part of the Indian River, near Titusville.

Although these particular ring-billed gulls had clearly developed a close relationship with brown pelicans, depending on them as a source of food, I generally view gulls as rather unremarkable creatures, consuming anything that is available. Ring-billed gulls, for example, commonly fly far inland to hang around garbage dumps where they scavenge food. Their numbers, in fact, have increased with the ever-increasing amount of garbage and number of garbage dumps we produce. But on rounding a bend of the ICW, a flock of laughing gulls reveals our ignorance of their culinary adaptability. The whole river is blocked by a tight raft of several hundred of the small, black-headed birds. They dip their bills shallowly into the water, constantly moving and swallowing. We slow down and drift with them while looking closely at the water's surface, where we see thousands of winged ants, unable to rise because their wings are trapped in the surface tension. They must have swarmed from their underground nests on one of the small islands to mate and colonize new islands, but a contrary wind cast them onto the water to drown or be devoured by the birds. All the energy and nutrients devoted to producing those ants are lost to the ant colony, but the gulls and fish benefit from the ants' loss. Who would have predicted that laughing gulls would feast on ants while floating in a salty river? The connection exists, even in its apparent improbability.

Farther into Florida we begin to see a few manatees. They are such gentle creatures, friendly as pet dogs, but they float at the surface and frequent the same channels that humans in fast boats claim as their own. They usually swim just below the surface, and we've followed the course of many a manatee by watching for the smooth, flat upwelling on the water's surface caused by the upward stroke of the huge, broad tail. Similarly, dolphins sometimes make small eddies if they are swimming slowly near the surface. All of the bigger manatees carry the scars of propellers on their backs, some with healed injuries that appear to be nonsurvivable from their extent.

We dock in a marina at Daytona Beach to take on fresh water and fuel. It is a convenient, protected location with little current to negotiate. While there, we see a manatee that comes in to investigate freshwater runoff from another boat's air conditioner. After drinking its fill, the manatee approaches the dock where I am sitting and positively asks to be scratched between the eyes and on top of its head. I comply even while Ed wonders whether it is a good idea. It is big and it is an endangered species, but clearly this animal has interacted with humans before. It closes its small, watery eyes in pleasure and remains absolutely stationary until I am exhausted from scratching.

Its gentleness seems surprising in such a large animal, but cows are gentle, too, when they are on the other side of a fence.

Manatees collect in areas of freshwater runoff and investigate any small rivulet that they find, as a thirsty person would after swimming all day in the salty sea. At the marina, someone dropped a hose into the water and left it drizzling freshwater. Another big manatee quickly found it, pulled the hose into its mouth with thick, whiskered lips, and drank gallons of it. It rolled onto its back with front flippers crossed across its chest, the hose dangling from its lips, like a tethered dirigible or a mustachioed fat man reclining on a beach float with a straw in his drink. Ed and I sit up on the bow and watch the manatee. It lingers, drinking from the hose until we grow bored and stand up, which startles the creature and causes it to move away.

But it doesn't go very far, swimming over to another dock face to graze algae growing there. To feed, it uses its lobed upper lip, which is modified so that each side is very flexible, almost prehensile, and with short, stiff whiskers on this lip, it plucks algae and guides them to its mouth. Ed tries to move his own mustachioed lip in a similar fashion, but it is impossible to do so, and we both laugh at the silliness of it all. Manatees feed on algae, but move so slowly that algae grows on their skin, coloring them slightly brownish-green like the slow-moving sloths of South America, which grow algae in their fur.

Early one quiet morning, while at anchor near Fort Pierce, Florida, we watch a mother manatee and her new calf. The youngster is about three feet long, gray, and smooth-skinned, too youthful for algae to have yet gained hold. The front flippers of both manatees, although shaped like fingerless, flat paddles, are adorned with finger-nails, revealing their evolutionary relationship to land animals with fingers and toes. While the mother hangs in the water, occasionally moving just enough to put her nose above water to take a breath, the little manatee explores its environment without straying more than a few feet from its mother's side. It occasionally nuzzles into its mother's armpit for a mouthful of milk, sometimes dribbling a stream of the white liquid from a corner of its mouth. At other times, it grazes algae from its mother's back, moving like a cleaning shrimp over a large grouper. The adult manatee provides a surface for algae to grow on, and the algae are, in turn, eaten by her offspring.

Although most manatees we see swim in quiet waters of Florida's lagoons, we also get a glimpse of a very large manatee in the ocean just beyond the surf. We are sightseeing on land while visiting family in Daytona Beach, watching a group of surfers waiting to catch a wave to ride. Suddenly, a huge, dark shape looms up from the depths straight toward the most distant surfer. We are too far away to call a warning, but Ed and I look at each other, both thinking the same thing, and begin to run down from the dune we are standing on toward the water's edge. Just before we frighten the entire population of surfers, fishermen, and swimmers by screaming "Shark!," the giant shape sticks its head above water and materializes into a manatee. Chagrined, we are justified in our vivid imaginations just a few weeks later when a big shark is caught from the nearby pier, and surfers stay away for a while after that.

While docked at the marina in Daytona Beach, we take the opportunity to visit the area by car with our relatives. Nearby is Tomoka State Park, and as we drive along the road that cuts through the park we are astounded by the little piece of old forest that survives there. Enormous live oak trees hang over the road and shade it from the intense sun. They shelter lengthy growths of resurrection fern whose fronds sprout from the branches like feathers on a bird wing, hairy clusters of Spanish moss that dangle in the breeze like thin gray goatees, and clumps of native orchids on the thickest branches. The understory is clogged with palmetto shrubs and so wild that it looks as if a rattlesnake should be slithering along the sandy forest floor at each step I take toward the interior. Here, too, the Timucuan were the local tribe, preserved in the name of the park.

It takes us a couple of weeks to move through Florida, sightseeing, visiting friends on land, and generally just enjoying our trip. Soon enough, we find ourselves in southern Florida, where we spend a long weekend anchored in Lake Worth near Peanut Island.

The anchorage is close to the short, deep inlet, and on a rising tide we watch clear, Gulf Stream water flow past. On more than one incoming tide, we don diving masks and hang below the surface on the anchor chain. Once, a huge southern stingray larger than I am glides beneath us, and later a big barracuda hangs suspended just underneath our keel. We swim with them both, although we respect their space and do not move too threateningly close. They do the same. At other times, as the clear, warm current flows past us, we open glass jars to collect delicate jellies and the oceanic larvae of many types of animals. In addition to fish and crab larvae that resemble their adult forms, we also catch spectacular larvae of creatures such as acorn worms, brittle stars, sipunculans, and sea squirts, whose crystalline clarity is more varied than snowflakes and whose animated forms are as diverse and engaging as the most beautiful flowers. We spend hours with microscopes and dishes of seawater, full of living creatures.

Delighted with the finds, we excitedly converse in a language of biology: "I have a metamorphosing tornaria here! This dish is full of so many ascidian tadpoles and larvaceans that I can't tell them apart! Wow, what's this gigantic [one millimeter], orange, swimming blob? It's a zoantharia larva! Come look at this: a transparent chaetognath has just eaten another one, and I can see the eaten inside the eater!"

We can't get enough of the clear water and interesting animals, sitting on deck only long enough to eat a sandwich and dry off slightly. We snorkel around Peanut Island, riding the current in and then back out to *Velella* while using slack tide for most of our snorkeling. She waits patiently, swinging slowly on her anchor to face the inlet on the rising tide and Peanut Island as the tide falls.

We discover an amazing number of colorful animals, each causing momentary panic as we try to speak through our snorkels. Beautiful file clams, a type of scallop with a reddish-orange mantle extending into long tentacles of soft, colorful tissue that protrude from the two ordinary-looking valves of the shell, wedge into protective crevices of rock with only the tips of the orange tentacles extending. A huge orange reticulated sea star crawls across the sandy bottom toward the refuge of the clams. I wonder if it smells lunch. These sea stars are much less common than they once were, because they are large, beautiful, hold their color and shape when dead and dry, and they live in shallow, accessible, warm water. An old, large toadfish is so well camouflaged that I nearly mistake it for a rock to inspect until its eye turns toward my approaching hand; it waits patiently for a similar mistake from a small, edible fish. A dozen brilliantly colored splashes of orange, purple, white, yellow, and gray resolve into separate colonies of sea squirts and sponges covering the underside of the same rock. Although very distantly related animals, they are nearly indistinguishable from each other, and most people, seeing that superficial resemblance, would think they are the same. What a vibrant, multicolored, unseen, and unknown world of interactions just a few inches below the sea's surface!

The human inhabitants of our anchorage are no less interesting on this busy weekend. We had inadvertently timed our travel to Lake Worth to coincide with the Fourth of July holiday. In traveling the marshes, we have been seeking freedom from the mundane, yet find that this symbolic day of freedom is filled with rather ordinary people acting extraordinarily. We arrive in the anchorage a couple of days ahead of the weekenders, allowing us to occupy a secure area in the midst of the busy harbor. By Saturday afternoon, July 3, the anchorage bustles with all manner of boats: dozens of small powerboats, several large cabin cruisers, a few scattered sailboats, and a little converted tug anchored just ahead of us.

Boaters fall off their boats, swear loudly at each other's ineptitude, dive after anchors thrown over before being tied off, raucously laugh about someone else's poor anchoring ability as their own boat drifts slowly out of the harbor on the ebbing tide, and in general, make jolly fools of themselves. And that is just getting anchored! Then the captain of the tugboat promptly leaps overboard and calmly swims two hundred yards to shore, through the crowded harbor, while boats speed by him on all sides. We are still curious as to how he found his boat later that evening, in the dark, with an outgoing current and a long distance to swim, but a light appears in his cabin that night without the sound of an engine nearby.

One of the most outlandish sights is the competition between two outrageously decorated, barely floating hulks that pass for floating (or nearly so) hot-dog stands. "Henry's Grill" advertises hot dogs, hamburgers, and french fries fresh off the grill, evidenced by smoke that billows off the stern, and is bedecked with flags, streamers, and billboards. Not an inch of space is unoccupied by advertisements or decorations. Although Henry begins early, a competitor soon eclipses him by anchoring strategically upcurrent of Henry and sporting a bikini-clad sunbather prominently placed on deck. Soon this competitor has all the business, and Henry pulls up anchor to locate a new site. Dozens of Jet Skis, small powerboats, and even a large sportfisher temporarily tie up to the floating grill, but then buzz off, stomachs and eyes full of the fare.

At last, the long weekend over, most of the boats and their owners return to their land-based world, unaffected by their afternoon on the water except perhaps by lingering sunburn, while we, and the creatures just below our keel, continue to respond to the water's ebb and flow. Although planktonic animals we collect in our glass jars float northward, driven by the powerful Gulf Stream, we plan to travel eastward, cutting across the current's natural flow as we make passage across the Gulf Stream to the Bahamas.

Ed and I spend the afternoon and evening in a check of *Velella*'s readiness for sea, her sails, engine, and navigational equipment all carefully examined. We double-check that our passports are in the navigation table along with some cash in our wallets. With our final dinghy trip ashore, we load our fridge with the luxury of ice, then stow the dinghy and call it an early evening. Tomorrow we begin a new adventure, a separation from the safety of the waterway and an embrace of the unknown possibilities of the open ocean.

Bahamas

IT IS A MOONLESS NIGHT AND WE ARE ANCHORED NEAR WEST End, in the Bahamas. Although there are lights on the island, the sea is inky black. We are on deck, watching a glorious show of living fireworks explode in the water. It is a dance of the Caribbean palolo worm, and we have come to see it. The juvenile worm is unremarkable, attractive with its opalescent sheen, but nothing stunning. They live buried in sediment, and it is only when they mature and reproduce that fireworks begin.

At exactly fifty-six minutes after sunset, for two or three days after the full moon of each summertime month, such as this lovely July, tiny patches of green light start to appear at the surface as far as the eye can see. Each patch is a small circle of steady green light emitted by a female worm as she swims. Suddenly, deeper in the water, strongly flashing green lights rush toward the green circles from all directions. These are males, called "blinkers," and they are in a race to reproduce—first males win. When these fastest males reach a female, together they explode as they release their bioluminescent gametes. The green glow fades as fertilized eggs drift away.

The exploding worms are actually just parts of a larger worm. The real worm remains in its burrow, experiencing its own reproduction vicariously. Only the tip of its tail, which holds gametes, swims unaided to the surface, there to release gametes on cue. Within a month, if food is good, the worms have grown another kamikaze portion and fireworks begin again. Lights distract lovers, but at fifty-six minutes after sunset for two or three days after the full moon, the sky is absolutely dark. The worms are most active during summer months when the water temperature is warm enough to encourage fast growth and reproduction.

The worms perform just as expected, and we talk excitedly about other tropical islands that show such fantastic spectacles. These worms are a small species, but those that live near islands in the South Pacific, such as Fiji, Solomon, Cook, Samoa, Tonga, and Vanuatu among others, are so large, numerous, and conspicuously reproductive that islanders collect them to eat, thinking that they are a natural aphrodisiac. Reliable data regarding this effect are regrettably lacking, but Rafael Steinberg reports that, "With the first taste of palolo I understood the Samoans' love for it. Certainly it suggested a salty caviar, but with something added, a strong rich whiff of the mystery and fecundity of the ocean depths."

The Bahamas provide not only an exploration of a new, not-too-distant land, but a new experience of open ocean sailing. The trip from Lake Worth in Florida to West End in the northern Bahamas requires only one day, but necessitates that we use both sail and engine. Still, in one day we cross one of the great ocean currents on Earth, the Gulf Stream, and arrive in another country. Who could resist including the Bahamas as part of a cruise of the Southeast?

The Bahamas, however, are not part of the Southeast either biologically or culturally speaking. As we approach the low-lying Bahama Banks, the water of the Gulf Stream is bluer than the sky and looks infinitely deep. Not until we are in port can we see the bottom, and then it is suddenly, and uncomfortably, close. The water is so clear that I can scarcely believe the depth-sounder; I keep expecting to feel us scrape the bottom.

We left Lake Worth at 3:00 A.M. The short inlet was well-marked and calm, making for an easy exit. If the inlets farther north were as comfortable as Lake Worth Inlet, I would have nothing at all to fear. By leaving so early, we arrived on the Banks with plenty of time in the day. It also meant that we crossed the Stream during night, morning, and early afternoon, before the afternoon trade winds kicked up a sea. Still, the crossing is bumpy. With little wind, we motor-sail. To account for the strong set of the current, we angle sharply to the southeast, and I make frequent checks of the GPS (global positioning satellite system) and our charted position.

About halfway of the sixty miles across, we are stunned to see a small open fishing boat pulling rapidly up to our stern. As he pulls alongside, the captain asks if we are sailing for West End and if we are on course. When we reply in the affirmative, he pulls away, shouts a thanks, and heads on across the waves. Ed and I just look at each other without saying a word, both of us hoping that the guy makes it safely to harbor without flipping the small boat.

We pound through waves, often slapping down hard as our bow punches across their tops. In the last few miles, enough wind picks up to blow salt spray across the entire boat and halfway up the mast, where it dries into a white crust. The low island is tantalizingly close.

It is late afternoon when we arrive, which leaves us several hours to check through customs and get anchored. We mistakenly assume that the authorities will come rushing out to meet us, so we anchor in the harbor and proceed to restore some order to the chaos that has crept in below deck.

Immediately after setting the anchor in the shallow anchorage, we dive over to check it. The bottom is hard, white sand, and the anchor can find nothing to bite into. I push it into a slight depression, try my best to set it, and resurface. When I dive again on the anchor, I hang on the rope rode and watch a dozen electric-blue little fishes nibbling around the disturbed sand. Upon returning on deck and checking the depth-sounder, I am astonished to see it read almost eleven feet of water. I can see every fish on the bottom by looking over the side of the boat! Believing only my eyes, I double-check the sounder with my lead line. It is right! This is truly gin-clear water and a hard, white sand bottom. Are we really only sixty miles from the Southeast?

After an hour in the anchorage, I have replaced most of the gear that has shaken loose into the cabin, Ed has cleaned up the engine, bilge pump, and other vital instruments, and both of us feel that our kidneys have returned to their normal position in our bodies instead of up near our throats. Wanting no quarrel with the authorities, we motor into the docks and find the customs office after realizing they are not coming out to us.

The customs officer offers the ubiquitous "No problem, mon," as an answer to everything, but he is thorough. He checks through everything on board, looking underneath pillows and into cabinets. With no firearms to declare and no desire to buy a fishing license, we have only to pay the entry fee and port tax. He tries to talk us into renting dock space by describing some of the amenities in town, but we are only curious about the availability of water to rinse the salt off the boat. Freshwater, however, is charged by the gallon on this tiny island barely emergent from the salty sea.

As if on cue, another local arrives, also dressed in neat khaki shorts and shirt but lacking shoes. He is drumming up business for a nearby restaurant, and tries to entice us with a menu. Improbable in its burgundy backing, gilt lettering, and golden cord, the menu is carefully unpacked from a plastic slip cover stowed in the wire basket on the driver's bicycle. We handle the menu carefully as we look over it briefly, but tired from the crossing, anxious about holding in the hard sand, and impatient to see the luminous worms, we return to the anchorage instead of visiting the restaurant. Both of us feel that we've disappointed the fellow as we watch him pedal dejectedly down the sandy road back into town. In an instant we had been transformed from slightly crazy biologist-boaters to wealthy American tourists, and we suddenly realize that here, both descriptions are true.

Anchored again in nearly the same location, I use a single bowl of freshwater to wipe down the bronze hardware but feel too wasteful to rinse the whole boat. The water in our sun shower is already warm, for its black backing had been absorbing the summer sun's heat all the while we cleared customs. Ed hangs the shower over the mainsail's boom for me, and I hunker down in the cockpit to shower in the bathtub-like enclosure. Between the two of us we splash enough water to rinse the salt off the area surrounding the cockpit. I cook supper while Ed restores the cockpit to its more normal function, and we sit there to eat.

Clean now, recovered from the rough crossing, and full of supper, we watch the sun set and count the minutes. Luckily for us, there are enough worms in our anchorage to give us quite a show on the first night, and we are pleased that we've timed our trip correctly. After a day or so here at West End, we will travel farther around the Banks. We plan to stay a week or two.

We sit up until late in the night, even after the worms have ceased their frenzied dance. The air is so clear that the stars seem nearly within reach. The trade winds sweep across the ocean from the east, leaving the air clean of most pollutants or dust, and the difference between this clean air and the air of the east coast is noticeable. As we sit securely at anchor, enjoying the evening, several other boats come in from the crossing. They obviously left much later in the morning than we had. Clearly we made the right decision in starting early so that we could rest easily in our arrival. No way would I want to be coming into this anchorage at dark.

Our second day in the Bahamas dawns clear and breezy, so we set the sails, leave the anchorage, and then turn back onto the Banks in a channel that cuts through them. Or, at least, that is the plan. Another big difference between the ICW and the Bahamian channels is the lack of markers. Naively, we miss the channel by about five feet and come up hard onto the bank.

We hit so hard that *Velella* actually shudders. We both leap to our feet. I douse the sails, which are driving us farther up, while Ed cranks the engine. We try to power off, to back around, to somehow break loose, but we can't. To make it worse, the tide is falling. For hours, we grind and pound against the hard bottom, *Velella* creaking and flexing like never before. Waves roll in from the sea onto the banks, but each wave only sets us more firmly instead of releasing us. We watch in horror as a thundercloud builds, dark and massive, to the east of our position, but it moves away from us, thankfully. We spend a sickening day listening to *Velella* thump against the bottom. I thought we might lose her—and to a silly mistake.

Early in the afternoon, when the tide finally reaches low and begins to rise, a local boater motors out to help us. He pilots a flat-bottomed fishing boat, well used and full of gear, but with two powerful engines. First, he tries to tilt us over by pulling on one of the halyards, but only succeeds in breaking the halyard where it passes through the metal guides at the mast-top. *Velella*'s great weight pins her firmly to the bottom. He suggests that he could try the other halyard, but we politely refuse, recognizing that we will lose the ability to reach the mast-top if he breaks the second halyard. At last, he gives up, but not before towing out our anchors to set them in the channel. We give him a little money in payment for his time, and he leaves us with shouts of encouragement. "The tide is rising!"

We tighten up the anchor rodes and wait. I sit beside the rodes, resting a hand or foot on them, my eyes shaded from the intense sun by a broad-brimmed hat. As soon as they slacken at all, I tighten them. Inch by inch, I slowly gain back the rodes. As the tide keeps rising, we begin to slip along the bottom toward the channel. After nearly seven hours, we finally have more water than we had upon grounding, and we pull ourselves off the bank and into the channel. At last, we are free.

Chastened, we return to the anchorage late that afternoon and dive over to inspect the damage. A section on the keel nearly two feet square is gouged rather substantially. Probably a lesser boat would have been lost, but *Velella* pulled through even though both Ed and I considered that she might not. Unfortunately, however, one of our anchor rodes was abraded through by coral, and we have left one expensive anchor sitting in the channel. We have GPS coordinates for the grounding, and realize that the anchor will be nearby, so we make plans for a salvage operation.

In a stroke of very bad luck, our dinghy motor refuses to work. Ed spends much of our third day in the Bahamas in trying to repair the motor, but to no avail. Our anchor spends another night in the channel, and *Velella* stays in the anchorage. A boater near us notices our plight and comes over that evening in his dinghy.

"Problems with the motor, there?" he asks.

"Yes, and I'm stumped by the cause of it," Ed replies.

The captain offers a few suggestions, but Ed has already tried all the obvious repairs and nothing has worked. The motor has been running fine all during our trip along the ICW, but here, where we must have it, it fails. We figure we will have to hire someone to find the anchor, and probably pay as much as the anchor itself is worth.

In the community spirit that is common to most boaters, our comrade promptly offers his dinghy for us to use in the morning. "Look," he says, "I'll come over right after breakfast. If you have the coordinates, it should only take us a few minutes to find it."

True to his word, he appears the next morning in his substantial inflatable dinghy, and we zip over to the coordinates. Ed jumps over with his flippers and mask, and within a few minutes has located the anchor rode, which he pulls on board. I am ecstatic to have him back aboard too, as I was uncomfortably remembering scenes from *Jaws* as he swam around in the channel. We haul up the anchor without incident, return to the big boats, and hand over a case of beer in gratitude. We have spent four days in the Bahamas without moving more than a few hundred, and hard, yards!

That evening, we discuss our options. "How much damage did we do to the keel?" I ask Ed after returning from a dive to check it. It looks raw and ragged to me.

"It's hard to tell, but we compromised the epoxy barrier and will soon start taking on water as it soaks through the fiberglass. I'm afraid the freshwater tank may have sustained some damage, too."

The hundred-gallon tank was positioned in the bilge, just above the point at which we'd hit the bottom.

"We need time to explore these islands," I say. "They're so clearly part of the Caribbean instead of the Southeast. Another week won't get us very far around here. A month would be better."

"I agree," Ed replies, "but I don't think we should wait that long to haul out and make repairs. I don't want to be caught on the other side of these islands if we start to have serious problems. At the very least, we're likely to start taking on water through the hull. If the water tank is cracked, we'll lose our freshwater, too. Besides, another grounding on this abrasive bottom would not be good for her."

"You're right. We really ought to head back. It will take us at least a week, anyway, to get back to Beaufort and get hauled out."

"Yes," Ed sighs, "this trip is nearly over, but that doesn't mean we can't come back, with more time and more careful boating! We need to replace that broken halyard yet. You willing to ride the chair this time? Should be quick and easy!"

At the top of the mast, I have a great view of the harbor. I can even see over to where the channel we just missed is actually located. When I arrive back on deck, I tell Ed that maybe he should pull me to the top of the mast for any other Bahamian adventures, for it certainly made the navigation much easier.

"It seems that everything about the Bahamas is different from what we expected. Well, everything except for the worms!"

It has only been four days, but we are packing up again for a trip across the Gulf Stream. This time there will be no motor-sailing because we have the current with us and a fresh wind has piped up. Our sails will power us home. We should sail into a harbor on the east coast sometime in the next few days.

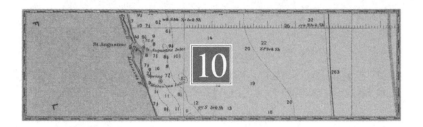

Gulf Stream to
St. Augustine

FINALLY FREE ON THE OPEN OCEAN WITH HUNDREDS OF
feet of water beneath our keel, I breathe a sigh of relief. We have
just left the Bahama Banks behind us, and I can still see the water
tower of West End, Grand Bahama Island, in the distance. Although
our short stay there was interesting, we had unfortunately come to
the jarring conclusion that enthusiasm coupled with inexperienced
navigation make a poor combination when sailing over the shallow
Banks. We agree with that greatest of fictional sea captains, Horatio
Hornblower, whose comment about the Banks was to "be careful of
your navigation there."

This journey will be a true passage, days and nights of sailing on
the heart of the great current of the Gulf Stream. This adventure
should give us a taste of open-ocean sailing, and if the taste becomes
unpleasant, a sharp turn to the west will get us into a port on the
Florida coast before things can really turn sour. All our previous day
sails along the southeastern coast were coastal cruising, the shore
just over the horizon, another boat almost always in view, the water
with a decidedly brownish tint, and we were hungry for more. Even

our daylong crossing from Florida to the Banks was a brief motor-sailing interlude, but now we are making a sailing passage. After this test, our next port of call can be any exotic destination we imagine.

With the Bahamas almost in our backyard, we could hardly ignore them as we took our first steps toward independence. They were another country! Like most sailors, we dreamed of seeing the world from the deck of our own boat and hoped that this step might be part of a greater adventure.

The Bahamas even have a historical connection to Charleston. After the Revolutionary War, when Charleston was an important port blockaded by the British, Loyalists to the British Crown left the city along with British troops. Some of them settled in the Abacos, the northernmost islands in the Bahamian chain, and tiny Man-O-War Cay is still populated mainly by the descendants of a group of these Loyalists. Although we didn't get all the way to Man-O-War during our sailing adventure, we have visited several times by air and then ferry, and we love the island, its biodiversity, and its friendly and orderly people. If we could figure out how to do it, I think we would move there permanently.

The Gulf Stream has an aura of mystery even though the great current has been extensively studied. Its path was traced long ago, and Benjamin Franklin published a map on which the Stream is correctly placed. The current flows northward out of the Gulf of Mexico through the narrow Strait of Florida, is deflected farther out to sea by Cape Hatteras, and then, as the North Atlantic Current, passes directly by the British Isles to bathe them with what is left of its warmth and moderate the entire climate of northwestern Europe. The latitude of London is about the same as the northern tip of Newfoundland, and it is the warmth of the current that makes London temperate the year-round. The great Atlantic Gyre continues to turn, however, and the warm current continues south, renamed the Canary Current as it passes by those islands, until it reaches the latitude of the trade winds, turns westward as the North Equatorial Current, and returns to its birthplace in the Gulf of Mexico.

One reason the North Atlantic Gyre is so well studied is because of the effect it had on sailing ships during the great Age of Sail. Most ships that sailed westward across the Atlantic from Europe first headed south to catch the North Equatorial Current and the trade winds, which carried them to the Antilles. This was the route Columbus took when he landed on Hispaniola, a large island now shared by Haiti and the Dominican Republic, and subsequently on other Caribbean islands. Later, the Spanish took possession of many Antillean islands as well as the mainland of Florida. From there, their supply and trading ships traveled northward, using the Gulf Stream to assist them just as we were. Similarly, the earliest English explorers arrived first in the West Indies before sailing north to make landfall at Roanoke Island in what is now North Carolina, and their ensuing explorations continued to use that route, which is much longer in miles, but more propitious for sailing than a direct shot from England to North Carolina would be. In addition to advantageous sailing conditions, the indirect route offered the opportunity of plunder of Spanish ships and quick escape to the north. Many of the British who colonized Charleston first settled on the Caribbean island of Barbados, which achieved independence from Britain in 1966. It was their profitable experience in the slave-based plantation economy of Barbados that committed Charleston to the same fate.

Quite apart from its value to colonial, as well as contemporary, sailors, the Gulf Stream is also the lifeblood of uncountable numbers of animals; it is a great artery that is home to many of them, provides food to others, and is an aid to reproduction of still more. Both eggs and larvae are carried by the current to new locations, far beyond the distances that their parents could swim or crawl. Some animals spend their entire lives afloat in the current, but others are wanderers only as youths; they drop out of the current and settle to the bottom as they transform into adults. Tiny larval fish are caught in the tentacles of oceanic jellies, which are in turn swallowed by larger fish that come and go in the current. A larval crab is trapped by the feathery feet of a goose barnacle, eaten by a crustacean cousin, but when the goose barnacles are blown ashore, attached to floating bits of wood or bright plastic, the ghost crabs descend on them to change the bits of barnacle back into ghost-crab larvae.

And we do see bits of plastic and other flotsam by-products of humanity even out here in what feels like unspoiled space. Pieces of floating plastic that blow off a Caribbean island could end up on the shoreline of England or even back on a Caribbean beach, for that is the direction of the current. The Sargasso Sea forms in the relatively unswirled center of the North Atlantic Gyre, like the calm eye of a hurricane around which the winds rotate. Seaweed, the floating species of *Sargassum*, occupies this central eye where the current is slack, but so too does a bewildering array of floating refuse from our shores. We see plastic bottles, plastic bags, Styrofoam floats from fishing nets, plastic and wooden shipping pallets, and varying pieces of unidentifiable plastic.

The oceanic eye is called the North Atlantic Garbage Patch (there is another in the Pacific Ocean), and it is full of the accumulated debris from our society, but it is an important location for several animals as well. Juvenile sea turtles leave Atlantic beaches, fight through the Gulf Stream and the predators that cruise in it, and eventually find the Sargasso Sea, where they spend several years eating *Sargassum*, hiding in the seaweed from predators, and growing. Both American and European eels leave their freshwater streams when they reach adulthood, swim to the Sargasso Sea, and spawn there. Both sea turtles and eels are declining in number, perhaps because the juveniles are adversely affected by all the trash that has accumulated in their nursery grounds. Oceanic birds such as albatrosses can have so much plastic in their guts that they die from it; some scientists estimate that a third of their chicks die because the parents inadvertently feed them plastic when they regurgitate fish.

As the plastic pieces break down into smaller components, they still affect life. Filter feeders, such as the goose barnacles we see attached to floating plastic bottles, filter and swallow the miniscule fragments of plastic trash and the chemicals associated with their breakdown products. The plastic and pollutants collect, fouling their filters and their guts with indigestible plastic instead of nutritious particles. Many plastic by-products are estrogen mimics and are undoubtedly affecting the reproduction and development of oceanic invertebrates, fishes, birds, and mammals as well as the land-based species that are better documented.

We leave the Banks in the afternoon and immediately enter the Gulf Stream to find that the constant southerly wind over the last several days has blown up the seas a bit, but *Velella*, with her canoe stern, handles the following seas gracefully, and we ride up over them easily. With a single reef in the main and our jib flying, we tear through the water, leaving foamy bubbles in our wake. The wind is full in our sails, and we are free to fill all our senses. The sun shines over the crystal-blue sea, the wind caresses our faces, and we inhale fresh air that tastes of salt from the spray our heaving bow creates as we throb through the waves. As Whitman describes in "In Cabin'd Ships at Sea":

> The sky o'erarches here, we feel the undulating deck beneath
>   our feet,
> We feel the long pulsation, ebb and flow of endless motion,
> The tones of unseen mystery, the vague and vast suggestions
>   of the briny world, the liquid-flowing syllables,
> The perfume, the faint creaking of the cordage, the melancholy
>   rhythm,
> The boundless vista and the horizon far and dim are all here,
> And this is ocean's poem.

Late that evening, as we cross the central axis of the great Gulf Stream, the GPS reports that we are moving faster over the Earth's surface than ever before. Although we seemed to be moving at a pleasant but unremarkable rate, the distances between the dots on the chart that mark our location every four hours for the past twenty-four tell a different story. By riding the current, we speed along without the sensation of haste.

Because the sailing is so comfortable, one of us sleeps on deck while the other steers at the helm. Ed and I set up a schedule of two hours on and two hours rest during the nighttime. After completing my first watch, from ten until midnight, I awaken Ed, who has been sleeping on deck beside me. He takes the wheel and I lie down, but I remain awake. Prone to seasickness, we both wear scopolamine patches, and the drug affects Ed by making him drowsy. Strangely, it has the opposite effect on me. During the midnight until 2:00 A.M. watch, Ed struggles to stay awake while I lie on deck drifting in and out of sleep, awakening frequently. Finally, after an hour of nodding off and then abruptly waking, startled and worried that the boat has drifted off course, Ed asks me to finish his watch. I do, and stay at the helm until the first hint of dawn caresses the horizon.

That particular overnight sail is a revelation for both of us. In sailing, you rely on your crew. While one sleeps or rests, another is watching. While one steers, another handles sails or navigates. Ed and I learned to rely on each other as we learned to sail, but our Gulf Stream passage was the most intense learning experience. Giving up control is not easy, especially for strong individuals. Neither of us wanted to burden the other, but neither wanted to be so completely and obviously dependent on the other, either. In those few hours of being completely responsible for all of us, however, I realized that by caring for us as a unit, I was also developing personally. I was responsible for sailing and navigating, for watching the compass course, for adjusting the sails, and I had grown in my confidence and in the skills needed to operate the ship. At the same time, I became freer from my ego, no longer even attempting to determine whether my needs or our needs were different. They were the same.

By the time the sun is a few degrees off the horizon, Ed is awake and feeling less groggy from the effects of the drug. I am tired, but pleased with the job I have done. I turn the wheel over to Ed, go below to check the GPS position and use the head, and return on deck to find my husband grinning at me. "I thought you were nervous about steering the boat, Jennifer, but here we are and I've been asleep for hours. You did it! And thanks. I couldn't have done it without you, you know. Your turn to rest." So I do, lying down on the deck beside him, where I promptly fall asleep to the gently rolling swells.

Later that afternoon, I take the wheel again and give Ed an opportunity to relax. We abandon our schedule of two hours on and two hours off, preferring to recognize and adjust to our needs instead. Almost as soon as I sit down behind the wheel, a big, black shape looms up inside a rolling wave just off our starboard bow. Excited, I call to Ed, and we strain our eyes for another glimpse of the creature. "A whale!" I shout. "That was a whale! Look at that thing! I've never seen one in the ocean before!" Unfortunately, we could never figure out what kind of a whale it was, other than one of the smaller, black types, and I realize now why the old sailors put all of the small, black whales into a group called, generically, blackfish. It was enough to describe them thus. I spent the rest of my watch looking in every direction for another.

We didn't see another whale or even the spout of one. Whales are much less common than before the whaling industry decimated them. Whales are long-lived, slow to reproduce, and their numbers were so reduced that they are having a hard time recovering even though an international moratorium on whaling was established in 1986. Several countries, most notably Japan, have ignored the moratorium and continue to kill whales for their meat although they claim it is for scientific research. Formerly, whales were so common along the entire eastern seaboard that villagers could see the whales from shore and put out from the shore to harpoon them, as described in John Hay's books and elsewhere. The large whales are still critically endangered, but some of the smaller species including various types of dolphins are making a comeback. As their numbers increase, however, the clamor for renewed whaling is growing from Japan, Iceland, Russia, and various indigenous groups in the United States, Canada, and Indonesia.

On one of my trips belowdecks, I check our small library and am relieved to see that we have a copy both of Melville's *Moby Dick* and Murphy's *Logbook for Grace*. I've read them both before, but after actually seeing a whale, it will be interesting to read them again. I remember how Melville, in 1851, describes the sperm whales that they hunt and how they identify different species of whales based on the shape and size of the spouts. Murphy, writing about his experiences on a whaling brig in 1912, several times notes that the whales they killed were disappointingly small. By his time aboard, the whalers were taking younger animals because the larger, older ones were already gone. No wonder we see so few today.

Near evening, we are astounded to see birds that look like purple martins skimming along just over the wave crests and fluttering down into the troughs. What could purple martins, so common in midsummer's landlocked fields and pastures, be doing out here, sixty miles off the coast, with nothing but a watery perch to float on during the night? We have several close looks at the dark little birds, so similar in size and flight pattern to purple martins, but a glance at a field guide and a white flash just above the squared-off tail reveal them to be Wilson's storm petrels.

Again, the old sailors on square-rigged ships come to life. The little birds are called storm petrels because sailors saw them flying during storms, darting and fluttering across the wind-whipped waves; some even believed that their appearance predicted a coming storm. I hope not. The name petrel is also significant, referring to their habit, while hovering at the surface, to dabble their feet in the watery element; like the apostle Peter, they briefly walk on water. The birds are also sometimes called Mother Carey's chickens, an anglicized version of "Mater Cara," which is an invocation uttered to the blessed mother for protection by frightened sailors during violent storms.

Flying low overhead with strong wing beats that propel it endlessly through the air, a sooty tern closes the distance between us. Its cheery chirps and flight so close by the boat make it a welcome escort. Sooty terns look and act very much like the light-feathered terns of inshore waters, wheeling about in the air and, having spied a fish, diving recklessly after it, but their dark backs and white bellies are reminiscent of the patterning of skimmers instead of inshore terns. As night falls, a pair settles down on a floating piece of blue plastic that looks like part of a barrel, safe for a while from hungry predators below. Early the next morning, a different pair lifts off from a pallet of drifting wood and dives immediately after the small fish that share the protection of the floating platform. Their call, which sounds something like "wide-a-wake," seems particularly appropriate.

The wind drops off toward morning, and we drift gently along as we watch a spectacularly huge, red orb of a sun rise up out of the watery blue. We shake out the reef and unfurl the spinnaker, which keeps us moving ahead on the breathy gasps of wind. The waves have dropped to a lazy swell, and since we both feel more like eating, I head below to cook a pot of grits. Grits are a perfect food for southern sailors, comparable only to the Cream of Wheat favored by those from colder climates. Creamy, warm, and simple to cook, both are eminently soothing to a weary stomach, reassuring to the tired sailor, and do not require a long stint in the rolling galley.

While briefly heating water in the galley, a shout from Ed brings me dashing up the companionway, and I follow his gaze toward the water off the bow. There it swims, the terror of the deep, a dorsal fin and tail fin sculling slowly through the surface of the water. The shark, an estimated eight-footer, swims leisurely across the bow, checking for any discarded tidbits and then sinking from sight into the blue depths. We are suitably impressed, and cease to lean so far over the stern rail as we peer into the unknown.

"That shark seemed big, but it would be a minnow compared to *Megalodon*," I say to Ed. The fossilized teeth, the size of my hand, are collected from lowcountry fossil sites and phosphate mines, but are also found all over the world. A museum in the tiny town of Aurora, North Carolina, has an impressive plaster reconstruction of a *Megalodon* head among its many fossils and thousands of shark teeth that were recovered from the nearby phosphate mine. Each time we visit, I consider purchasing one of the gigantic teeth from the gift shop, but end up with some other type of fossil instead.

Ed replies, "We should be glad they are extinct. At only thirty-seven feet in boat length, we're probably in the size range of their prey."

"I read that *Megalodon* reached sixty feet in length and probably specialized on eating whales. Now that's a big shark!" I pause, thinking for a moment. "I wonder why they went extinct. There are still whales to eat."

"Maybe they didn't!" Ed says and hums the theme from the movie *Jaws*.

Deciding to experiment with offshore fishing, and determined to test my new surf rod-and-reel, I drop over a heavy, silver, cigar-shaped lure with a large, sharp hook attached. With a twelve-inch steel leader and sixty-pound test line, I thought I was ready to land anything that would fit into the cockpit of our boat. With the progression of the rising sun, winds return, and we are clipping along at about five knots under all sail when suddenly the line begins to sing. I leap up, grab the pole from the rod-holder, and Ed brings *Velella* into the wind to slow us down, but the line snaps before I can land the fish. It takes another attempt before I learn how to set the drag: too tight and the line pops as soon as the fish hits it; but too loose and the line could be stripped off before we slow the boat.

Quickly reaching a happy medium, however, I hook into one and begin to reel it in. The fish sounds, strips off line, and I slowly reel the line back on as soon as I can. Then it sounds again and we repeat the dance. This continues for some time, and as my arm begins to tire from fighting the twisting, bending rod, I suddenly see the fish down below. The water is so clear that I assume I will have the fish up on the boat in a second, but I must reel on forty and more feet of line before it is actually up to the boat. Again, it strips off line as it darts straight down into the depths out of sight—what is this thing? That is its last effort, however, and I finally reel in an exhausted barracuda with no fight left.

The barracuda is too large to fit in our landing net. Ed uses the gaff instead, and thinking to end it quickly for the fish, strikes with the gaff's sharp hook at the fish's head. The blow, however, glances off the impressively thick skull, and the end of the steel gaff, as thick as a pencil lead at the tip, bends ninety degrees! We land the fish by slipping the gaff-hook underneath the gill cover and lifting the fish aboard. It never fought once it was brought alongside the boat, its death struggle having been, apparently, the last sound into the depths. Even so, I immediately remove the head with those impressive daggers of teeth before retrieving my hook.

Now this is a fish! It fills the footspace of the cockpit, from which our feet are quickly removed, and extends all the way from the instrument panel back to the helm. A later measurement of this area is over four feet, and we guess the fish weighed twenty pounds. Although barracuda can carry the tropical fish disease ciguatera, as can most any fish of the tropical reef, a barracuda in the open ocean consumes the same food as dolphin fish and wahoo, and the flavor of barracuda is at least equal to that of those well-known game fish. We are kept in protein for the rest of our voyage and celebrate our good fortune over exquisite dinners of grilled, lightly gingered, barracuda steaks.

Ciguatera poisoning, however, is not a disease to be taken lightly, and Atlantic barracuda meat is not sold commercially for that reason. Since they are rarely eaten and commercially unimportant, the numbers of barracuda have remained stable even as the stocks of desirable, marketable fish have declined. It is hard to detect a fish containing the toxins that cause ciguatera, the toxins are not eliminated by cooking, and there is not a method of treatment for the digestive problems that result other than time. In severe cases, neurological damage may also occur from the toxins, which are produced by dinoflagellates, the same organisms that produce red tides. The toxins build up in the food chain so that top predators such as barracuda can contain dangerous amounts.

About a dozen strange growths cluster on the left side of the barracuda's head. They are shaped like goose barnacles, with an oblong portion of their body connected to the fish's skin by a thick, finger-like stalk. It is difficult to believe that they are living animals, for they hardly move, but they are parasitic crustaceans, related to goose barnacles as well as to crabs and shrimp. Their larvae had encountered this barracuda, somehow managed to gain a foothold on its slick and tough skin, then burrowed in to steal some of the barracuda's blood as they transformed into adults and reproduced more of their kind.

The most surprising fish we catch while sailing in the Gulf Stream is a remora. While sitting on deck, keeping an eye on my line, I see the remora swimming beside us, and point it out to Ed. We decide that it probably mistook *Velella*'s large, smooth belly for the belly of a shark. It soon realizes that the illusory belly is connected to a boat above, and drops off out of sight. When a fish hits my line, I suspect the remora, although I didn't really think it would strike at the big lure. Usually remoras eat pieces of whatever their shark host provides, but this lone remora, at least, is hungry enough to make an attempt at catching its own food. Reeling in the remora is like reeling in a lead weight; it is perfectly content to hang motionless, allowing me to drag it along as its shark host would have done, then just as it reaches the boat, it begins to swim strongly, and always downward. My arms are shaking from the constant effort when we finally, carefully reach behind its gill flap with the gaff and remove the hook from its mouth. We release the strange animal, its head flattened into a disk on top but the rest of its body remarkably like the shark it relies on to provide food, shelter, and means of travel.

Speeding along through the water while under full sail, we startle flying fish. I stand out on the bowsprit, which hangs over the water at the front of the boat and provides the sensation of flying over water. Three flying fish suddenly leap out of the water beside us, fly through the air, and drop back in again. They are as blue as the water and their fins are wide, like wings. Another one leaps up so high that it actually hits the lower edge of the jib and falls, startled, back into the water before its glide should have been finished. I've heard that some islanders catch flying fish to eat by fishing for them not with lines and hooks, but big sails instead.

Spotted dolphins frequent our wake and are among our favorite of Gulf Stream visitors. They come from far and wide, altering their courses to intersect ours and, as we imagine, jump for joy upon seeing *Velella*. Watching them leap completely out of their world and into ours, droplets of water cascading from their glistening gray bodies as they fall headfirst back into that bluer medium, we can hardly resist shouting joyfully ourselves. Such beauty, power, and energy they possess, riding our wake, darting out to chase a fish or another dolphin, then cutting across our bow, under the keel, around the stern, catching a breath beside us without ever slowing the pace. The offshore spotted dolphins are smaller and more compact than the bottlenose dolphins of inshore and are covered with white spots along their dark-gray sides.

They follow us even during the night, outlined by fire in the luminescent water. In the complete darkness of those few hours between the setting of the moon and the rising of the sun, I am alone at the wheel. Suddenly I see person-sized streaks of greenish light in the blacker darkness of water as dolphins converge rapidly on the boat. They ride beside me at the stern, startling me with their explosive breaths and eerily outlined bodies. Millions of bioluminescent, single-celled organisms are present in the water and respond to the movement of the dolphins by emitting light in a protozoan shriek of terror. What if I saw the illuminated tentacles of a giant squid hurtling toward us? The pod stays with us for over an hour before turning off at some crossroads unknown to us on the watery highway.

Cruise ships, too, follow a highway of sorts: the shortest distance between their home port and the large ports of the Bahamas. While we sail northward, riding the current, we encounter more than one heading south, plowing directly into the natural current. They run countercurrent to nature while we, on our small sailboat, use the wind and the current to move us forward. The cruise ship is bedecked in bright lights, sounds of rock music echo from its decks, and a thick cloud of smoke indicates the huge amount of fuel it is burning. We feel its wake although we are a mile away, as it pushes aside the water. Those engines generate an electrical current that keeps all those lights and speakers on. What happens when the engines stop and that current ceases to flow?

And speaking of energy, we are cruising happily along in the morning when a helicopter approaches us. It is fast, small, and dark, and once up close, we realize it is military. It practically buzzes us, and we wonder what in the world is going on. Has something happened since we left the Bahamas? I double-check the charts to ensure we aren't in a restricted area and turn on the radio to listen to the news, but nothing unusual is indicated. Ahead of us, however, we see something approaching, and quickly. We soon identify it as the conning tower and upper section of a nuclear sub, just as we'd seen in Charleston Harbor. This one is heading south, almost certainly out of the Kings Bay nuclear sub base. It disappears just as quickly as it had arrived, running at incredible speed. Later that night, we hear on the news that the president is in Miami, and we wonder if his presence prompted the sub's movements.

As we approach the shore in the late afternoon, we are rewarded with the sight of beautiful balloons of mixed shades of purple, pink, and blue, floating across the surface of the water. These gorgeously colored floats of Portuguese man-o'-war are being propelled by wind and current, just as we are, toward the north. As it would for us, a stranding on a wave-swept beach would bring the jellies to an unpleasant end, and I nervously hope that the GPS is right about our position. As we sail along beside the raft of jellies, individuals occasionally dip their sails into the water to counteract the effects of the drying wind. It is easy to forget that those gaily colored, seemingly inanimate balloons are animals, too, affected by their environment just as we are.

Approaching St. Augustine, the first structure we see is the distinctive black-and-white striped lighthouse on Anastasia Island. Not distracted, we keep our course toward the north until locating the first of the sea buoys, at some distance from the lighthouse. A sailboat behind us, also coming from the south, is convinced that the lighthouse must mark the nearby channel and starts a run directly toward it, but the breakers or his depth-sounder warn him back, and he follows us northward until the sea buoys come in sight. As we move slowly in through the winding, eel-like channel, with breakers clearly visible on either side, I comment to Ed that I am glad we have the sea buoys to mark the channel. "I wonder how often these buoys must be moved. I hope they are more accurate than those on the ICW around Matanzas Inlet."

"Yes," Ed replies, "can you believe that Spanish and English ships sailed through these very waters without the help of a motor, buoys, or GPS, in boats with a draft double and triple that of our own?"

"But at least they sent out their longboats first and rowed through the inlet before bringing in the ship, didn't they? They took more time then, but I guess they usually had the time. Instead of trying to get somewhere else, they were exploring right here. And their ship was their whole world—everything they needed right there with them for years at a time." I was pondering the implications of the early explorers when Ed cocks his head over to one side and glances at me.

"Jennifer, would you like me to take the helm? You're bringing us in the inlet yourself."

"I know. Weird, isn't it? This is probably the narrowest channel we've ever entered or left, and I don't like inlets. But everything is going so well that I'd like to continue and gain some more experience. So far, this inlet is easy. Okay with you?"

"Great with me!" Ed grins. "I think I'll go below and take a nap!"

"You will not!" I laugh at him. "Keep yourself right here beside me in case I need your help."

"Soon I'll just be a deckhand," Ed ribs me. "I don't know that I am entirely comfortable with you learning how to handle all aspects of this boat. You'll head off without me sometime."

"Don't worry," I chuckle. "I still can't fix the engine!"

"That's great. Grease monkey and deckhand aboard my own boat! At least I have something to do."

As we sail farther into the inlet and Matanzas Bay opens in front of us, the Castillo de San Marcos, a gray, weathered fort built of coquina rock, comes into view. Coquina rock was formed as millions of the shells of these delicately colored, tiny clams were ground into fragments by the force of the waves and then compressed into great cakes, cemented together by the pressure of seawater and sand above them, similar to the way tabby is formed from oyster shell. The rock for the fort was quarried on Anastasia Island, where the lighthouse is located. In sandy Florida, it was the only "rock" easily available for building forts or monuments.

The fort was built in 1672, more than one hundred years after the city was first founded, to protect Spanish interests against the English. It was needed, too, for in 1702, a group of English colonists from Charleston laid siege to the city. The fort was the only structure not taken by the English, and the arrival of Spanish ships saved the Spanish settlers and soldiers who had taken refuge inside it. The Spanish ships trapped English ships in the harbor, and the English burned their ships and escaped by land.

As we imagine menacing cannon and mortars on its ramparts and look back at the narrow channel through which we would escape if we were the threatened ship, the security of the Spanish position is clearly evident. Cannonballs at close range or wicked shoals both within and outside the bay were the choices faced by attacking ships before they could even bring a broadside to bear on the city. St. Augustine slowly slides into view, and the picturesque Bridge of Lions welcomes us as friendly visitors to the city.

As we edge slowly into the "holy-hole," an anchorage not far from the huge cross that commemorates the site of the first mission established in the New World, we can almost hear the ghosts from centuries past, Spanish, English, and Native American alike. I give up the helm and move onto the foredeck as we work together to set the anchor. The anchor chain rumbles out of its locker and we come to rest, tired from our passage but invigorated by our experiences, as equally tired and excited sailors have done for centuries. We have ridden one of the greatest natural currents on Earth.

Since we have such a good anchorage and are curious to learn more about the city, we stay in St. Augustine for a few days. We explore several well-known restaurants and try everything from French pastries to delectable paella and a bouillabaisse that makes us think we are in the Mediterranean instead of the United States. At one restaurant, we spend an hour entertained by flamenco dancers and guitar. But on a separate evening, we happen by a small bistro and are drawn in by the sounds of a gentle voice and folk guitar. The next afternoon, we bump into the same artist at a different venue and linger over lunch enjoying more entertainment. We are impressed and pleased by all the good music and lively atmosphere of the city. We even discover a wonderful bookstore that is packed with new and used books from floor to ceiling.

With so much food and fun atmosphere, we stay a week before we feel as if we have truly explored the city. With no evidence that our damaged hull is taking on water and no problems surfacing from our freshwater tank, our worries drift away on the tide. I feel different, more confident, more willing to just be where we are. To be somewhere else is not an urgent need, not even a simple desire. Crossing the Gulf Stream has been a rite of passage, one that we have successfully navigated. We aren't novices any more.

Tempest

AFTER A FEW DAYS IN ST. AUGUSTINE, FULL OF FANTASTIC food, great folk music, and volumes of books, with the memory of our Gulf Stream passage fresh on our minds, we prepare to leave through the same inlet we'd entered, on another offshore passage north to home. Glorious weather is forecast, with little chance of thunderstorms. We spend the morning preparing for sea, checking navigational equipment, stowing away everything that could bounce loose, filling up with fresh water, rigging jacklines that run fore and aft along the deck to provide handholds and lashings in case of heavy weather, and listening to the latest forecast. It still sounds good, and we anticipate an early departure, then two days of beautiful sailing weather.

By afternoon, however, a heavy squall blows in, and we are forced to suspend our preparations as the skies darken. Exposed to the river's fetch and formidable wind gusts, we are soon rocking fore and aft as short and choppy waves pass beneath us. Luckily for us, the wind is not opposed to the prevailing current, and our bow faces directly into the wind. Even so, an occasional gust hits us at a slight angle so that *Velella* is pushed over on her side for a moment before she rights herself. We are relatively secure in the holding power of our CQR anchor; in fact I fleetingly consider how difficult it will be for me tomorrow morning to break it out of the sticky mud bottom if the strain being placed on it is indeed burying it deeper.

A few sailboats and a small powerboat are heading up the river toward our anchorage when the squall strikes, and as we watch them struggle futilely against it, I can only praise the depth to which our anchor must be embedded in the bottom. They are headed directly into it, and the wind is so strong that one of the boats is actually losing ground, while others can only hold their position during the worst of it. The forceful wind lasts about a half hour, but then drops off as suddenly as it had arisen. As the opposing wind quickly fades, the small boats, with their engines still at full throttle, fairly fly up the river. The skies lighten, a gentle breeze springs up, and we smile to think that tomorrow will dawn with perfect sailing weather.

As promised, the next morning dawns clear and beautiful as we ride the current out of the inlet, motoring until we are offshore. Although the winds are predicted to reach fifteen knots, the air is now light and we set all sail. Throughout the morning and into the afternoon, we have a pleasantly lazy sail, with light wind. Puzzled about the lack of wind, we expect at every moment to catch those promised breezes. I fish for a while, but catch nothing, and switch to weaving rope lanyards for the shackles on the jib-sheet blocks. Whenever I tire of that task, I take the helm from Ed and he fishes for a while. It is an easy day and not at all the rapid transit we imagined.

As darkness falls that evening, the winds finally drop off to nothing. In the dead calm, we decide to crank up the Perkins diesel; such noise and bother, but it is better to be moving than just bobbing like a cork in the sea. We seem to be in a different reality than that of the weather forecasters, who continue to insist that we are having fifteen knots of wind. Motoring in a calm while the forecast calls for fifteen knots of wind is bad enough, but the noisy slap of slack sail against the rigging quickly convinces us to take in sail. We will be ready to reset it as soon as the wind arrives. While Ed steers, I douse the sails and clean up the lines, stowing them neatly so that the sails will be easy to reset. I also tie down the sails securely, since we are bouncing along and I don't want them to fly loose. I am doubly careful to make sure the halyard shackle is securely fastened, for we plan to raise those sails again just as soon as the wind comes up, and I have learned my lesson about loose halyards. Once everything is neat, organized, and secure, I turn back toward the cockpit.

As I move back from the deck to the cockpit, I call Ed's attention to a sharp line of black clouds behind us. "Just some thunderstorms heading out to sea," he says. "We should outrun them. They move from west to east off the land, and those are way to the south of us." I agree and don't worry. Another hour, however, and I am sure those clouds are gaining on us. "Impossible!" I think, but Ed and I watch despairingly as overhead, the stars wink out one by one.

I ask Ed if he recalls one of my favorite stories by Arthur C. Clarke in which the world ends once the monks of a peculiar religion have catalogued all the names of god. The chronicler is an unbeliever until the monks proclaim that they are finished and overhead, the stars begin to disappear. "It looks as if those monks have finally completed their task," I say, and Ed agrees, because, as in Clarke's story, "overhead, without any fuss, the stars were going out."

We are soon enveloped in the most spectacular show of natural energy ever imagined. Our retinas burn with the after-images of bolt after bolt of searing lightning; sometimes I can see both an after-image of one discharge and the actual strike of another. Incredibly bright flashes appear all around us, in every direction except dead ahead, where a few visible stars seem to pull us to hurry along. As if a lightning storm isn't electrifying enough, we are at least twenty miles offshore, on a boat with a fifty-foot mast, which is the tallest object for miles! We seem destined for a direct strike, and unplug all our electrical equipment to protect it from the powerful natural current that we are sure is to come. We wait for the illuminating flash, but no single bolt seems distinct from the others; they are all equally intense.

Instead, the wind arrives. It is fortunate the sails are furled, or they would have blown apart. We can see wind coming across the water, turning the oily smoothness of the sea's surface into a boil. We have just enough time to throw on our rain gear and latch down the hatches before the tempest is upon us. The front wall of the storm hits us as though the air has turned into a wall of concrete, rolling *Velella* on her beam ends until the starboard spreader tip, the cross-tree halfway up the mast, is dunked into the water. Nothing has done that before; it is a completely new experience for us all.

Ed elbows me and points forward with his head, unwilling to re-lease his grip on the wheel but trying to direct my attention. I search the deck and the water, concerned that something has gone amiss. He says, "look on the rigging there!" When another flash of light-ning illuminates the scene, I see a tiny anole, just a few inches long, gripping the vertical, stainless-steel shroud. The wind is blowing so hard that its tail stands out horizontally, like a flag. It is on the up-wind side and so was not dunked in the sea, but I doubt it can hold on much longer.

The bolts of lightning continue even as the wind increases. They come so fast, one upon the heels of the next, that the entire scene is illuminated. The brightness is not steady like the sun's, but comes in strobe-like flashes that make the experience seem unreal. The waves do not move constantly toward us but seem to advance piecemeal; one second there, the next second here, another flash and they have passed us. It is as if we are embedded in one of J.M.W. Turner's paint-ings, hopefully not *A Disaster at Sea*, but perhaps *Squall*. After a later perusal, I decide on *Dutch Boats in a Gale* as representative, even if we aren't Dutch.

The wind screams through the rigging, a high-pitched whine. Each metal wire plays like the strings of a demonical harp as the incredible wind rushes through. Unlike a harp, no dulcet notes are plucked. Instead, the noise grates on my eardrums like fingernails on a blackboard. My mouth floods with a sweet, familiar warmth. Confused, I touch my lip to find it bleeding, the red blood almost black in the flashes of light.

The tempest is overwhelming. Time becomes irrelevant; we exist only in the present as we are inescapably gripped by the moment. After an initial, searing flash of fear, I cease to be anxious. It is pointless to worry about the future when the present is so all-consuming. I dash below while Ed steers; there is nothing else for me to do but try to rest so that I can continue to function when I am needed.

I can hear rain pounding the hull beside my head. Since I am lying down in the quarter-berth, it means that the rain is blowing horizontally against us. We are heeled far over to starboard even though we have no sail set. The noise is so loud that it is all I can hear—raindrops hitting the hull with the force of stones hurled from the sky.

A second rogue gust knocks us down again. Below, the cushions and books not already scattered fly off the shelves, I am pitched against the doorjamb, and the heavy toolbox leaves its corner of the shelf to land an inch behind me. Aware that Ed is on deck without his safety harness and tether, I clamber up the companionway and peek out. He is there, latched onto the lifelines and steering wheel, his feet braced against the cockpit sides. He isn't going anywhere as long as a sea doesn't wash over. I am sorry that he lacks a harness, but there had been no time before, and it would be more dangerous now to try to get into it than to just hold on. We both hold on and wait.

After hours or minutes, I am unable to guess at which, Ed knocks on the overhead to signal a change in watch and I head up to the cockpit to relieve him. His hands are so stiff from gripping the wheel that I must help him to straighten his fingers before he can let go, slide over, and make room for me behind the wheel. Exhausted with the effort to keep *Velella* running with the wind and waves and himself on board, Ed promptly gives back to the sea what she has given him, then lies down and wedges himself in beside me, one arm wrapped around my leg. I check the clock on the way up the companionway and find that it is now 11:00 P.M.; the violence of the tempest lasted more than three hours, and now the boisterous wind has finally lost some of its aggression.

Once Ed has some time to recover, he takes the helm again and

I put on my safety harness, clip my tether to a jackline, and clamber forward to the mast to set the reefed main and reefed staysail. I am glad to have the lines already run and stowed neatly so that my excursion from the cockpit is a short one. I move like a crab, feet and hands always clutching or wedging into tight handholds or footholds. Although the teeth of the wind are dulled and no longer screeching through the rigging, the seas are a good fifteen feet high. We run before the wind and waves, cutting at a slight angle across them, even though it puts us a little off course. We will correct it later, and we really have no choice but to take what the ocean is willing to give.

I have some inkling now of the experiences that those hardened sailors lived through as they sailed the world's oceans. The intense wind, heavy rain, and the biggest seas I have ever seen threaten to pound us endlessly. When Richard Henry Dana rounded Cape Horn, he described enormous waves, forceful winds, and leaden skies, but eventually became so numbed to the conditions that he just wrote the poignantly simple repetition "the same" to describe daily weather conditions. We have just experienced a few hours of that awful sameness. We are both astonished that such a powerful storm was so long-lived. Such violent thunderstorms rarely last more than a half hour, but this one took three hours to blow through.

This tempest seemed to have been conjured up by Prospero and Ariel to deliver us to their shore. Perhaps we are being tested, as were the other visitors to Shakespeare's magical island. After all, his play was based on the wreck of the *Sea Venture*, when early colonists traveling from England to America discovered Bermuda after a violent storm blew them off course and so damaged their ship that the captain purposefully drove the ship onto the reefs in order to prevent it from sinking. They survived, salvaged the wreck, and built two new ships, eventually making it to the Jamestown colony in Virginia a year later, in 1610. Their delay in arrival may have even saved the struggling Virginia colony, for when the passengers and crew of *Sea Venture* finally appeared, most of the Jamestown colonists were sick or dead from disease and starvation. The exhausted colonists convinced the new arrivals to abandon the American colony and return to England, but on the very day of their departure, they were met by incoming supply ships and a hopeful few changed their minds and stayed. When the crew returned to England with fabulous stories of their rousing adventure and discovery of a bountiful island conveniently located, all of England was abuzz with excitement rather than focused on the near-disaster of the colony.

We later discover that the tempest was not a supernatural spell directed at us alone, but was a huge storm that affected many others. Some friends who were traveling the ICW with their dinghy in tow anchored for the night in a sheltered location. When the tempest hit, it flipped over their dinghy, ruining the motor, and as they wondered how they could ever right it, another gust picked up the dinghy and turned it right-side up. The tempest hit them at nearly the same time as it hit us, so it must have been at least thirty miles across, for they were anchored well inshore.

Throughout the night, the seas continue to ease, and by dawn are running at just five feet or so. By 9:00 A.M., the sun is once again shining on a blue sea, the waves are long, easy swells, and to cap it off, a beautiful wind of ten to fifteen knots springs up. So this is what we were supposed to have! How delightful, but how I wished the weather and the forecasters could have agreed.

We shake out the reefs and set the jib, sailing comfortably along. *Velella* acts as though she has actually enjoyed the challenge of the tempest and is now fairly leaping through the water. She was built to withstand that kind of weather, days of it, but it is heart-rending to take the test and wonder if she will survive it to pull us through. We are proud of our boat and pleased with her performance. We have survived our initiation as true sailors. No longer are we just dreaming; we are living in the adventure of sailing, accepting whatever is offered.

We sail in toward shore most of that day, since we are much farther offshore although also farther north than we had anticipated.

At least the tempest had come from behind, so that we continued to make forward progress. At the height of it, we were making eight knots under bare poles, with the engine on but at low idle.

By afternoon, the winds die off, we set the spinnaker, and we limp along until even the spinnaker ceases to fill with air. With the sails now slack, I move forward to make a repair. Several of the slides that attach the mainsail to the track running up the mast had torn loose. It left a couple of feet of the mainsail that did not attach to the mast, putting more strain on the points just above and below the defect. I get out a needle and heavy thread, put on my safety harness, clip myself to the mast like Ulysses, and then sew the slides back onto the mainsail. It's not the most beautiful job of sewing I've ever done, but when I checked my work later, back in port, I only needed to tighten up a stitch or two. We were back in business. Sewing on a loose button to a pair of pants or changing a car tire on dry land now seem simple in comparison to repairing a sail at sea.

Since we were nearing our home inlet, but lacking wind, we cut on the engine; we had finally learned enough about bumping slowly through inlets. However, we quickly develop a problem with the engine overheating. Ed discovers that he can run it for a while, rev it in neutral to cool it, then run it again while paying close attention to the gauges until it heats up, so we keep the routine as we head into the inlet. It is an imperfect solution, but it works, and we keep the engine from overheating. Ed steers, but I watch the gauges.

Once we are through the inlet and into the channel, I call ahead to the local marina, but the marina is full. "Do you think we can just keep going, Ed? We aren't far from our home dock and could just make the repairs when we arrive there, as long as we aren't damaging the engine."

"I agree," Ed replies. "If we just cut back on speed and give occasional rest periods to the engine, we ought to be fine on our own. Wouldn't you rather anchor out in a secluded, peaceful spot after last night's emotional highs and lack of sleep? I know I would!"

I agree wholeheartedly. There is, after all, no need for us to hurry

—we have left that lifestyle behind. Gladly, then, we search for an appropriate anchorage, and a beautiful stretch of spartina-flanked creek arises in front of us. Not a mile farther north is a slight elbow to the main channel, where a deep creek flows out of the marsh. We gently edge *Velella* into its mouth, sounding with a lead line until we are well out of the channel. We drop anchor gratefully. At last, to rest.

With the engine off, peacefulness returns. I hand a bucket of freshwater to Ed and, together, we wipe down all the bronze hardware and the cockpit area. Everything is covered in a crust of salt. As we are folding up the sails and wiping down the rigging, I startle our tiny lizard friend, who has found shelter underneath the wooden light-board on the shrouds. I am astonished that the flogging wind did not dislodge him and glad to see that he survived the tempest as well. No doubt his toes were as stiff from gripping the shrouds as Ed's fingers were from holding the wheel. I have a feeling that when we tie *Velella* in her slip, he may make a dash to freedom across the docking lines, which is probably how he arrived aboard. Ashore in a new port of call, perhaps he will woo lady anoles with tales of adventure on the high seas and introduce genes from the Florida anole population into Carolina.

We open all the hatches and let the fresh evening breeze blow through the cabin. We spend some time below, picking up books, tools, and all sorts of items that have flown from shelves or drawers. It looks as though the boat has just been picked up and shaken, based on the disarray of everything belowdecks. The most puzzling displaced item is one earring from a set that I had received shortly before our cruise began. I found it in the galley area, toward the after part of the cabin, but could find its mate nowhere. Several days later, the mate showed up in the V-berth, the forward-most part of the boat and a good fifteen feet from the site of the first one!

I finally clear a path to the stove to cook the first food either of us had been interested in eating for twenty-four hours. Ed, meanwhile, after washing down the critical parts of *Velella* and checking the engine and stuffing box, also washes down himself in a hot shower. I soon follow while Ed finishes the cooking, sharing in yet another task. What an experience that shower was! I stand while the blissfully hot water pours over my tired body, carrying away a thick layer of salt and sweat, rejuvenating my aching muscles and tender bruises. I feel the soreness and tension leave, emptying out through the soles of my feet, running down into the drain to be pumped overboard along with the salt that is returned to the sea.

We linger briefly over the meal to finish a glass of soothing port in the cockpit. Wading birds fly overhead to land on a small island just upstream in our little creek, where they also intend to stop for the night. The sky changes from pale blue to a glorious shade of orange and red. The few wisps of clouds pick up the orange, pink, and red tones and spread them across the whole sky, thickening the air itself into a tangible, golden hue, then briefly, just at sunset, the entire sky brightens momentarily to an intense, brilliant pink. It winks at us, acknowledging our transformation. The sky quickly fades into purple and slowly darkens to shades of gray, then darkness falls complete as we drain our glasses and slip below to the welcome softness of our bed. We can feel *Velella* tug slightly at her anchor chain, a gentle reminder of our surroundings.

Reflecting on the contrast between this evening's placid anchorage and last night's wild ride, we realize that they share a common theme. Each has been a direct and unaltered experience of nature, full of an intensity that produced a vivid set of memories. It took each of us, *Velella*, Ed, and I, to survive the tempest's test, and each of us had to grow, to learn more about ourselves as we developed new skills. Even *Velella* had a new experience of being knocked down to the water! Our egos were stripped away, and we emerged as a team, completely dependent on each other; a group of three transformed into one, but yet with our own personalities intact and improved. Prospero's magical spell had worked for us as well as for Ferdinand and Miranda; like them we emerged from the challenge harmoniously united.

Yardwork

ALONG WITH ALL THE ENJOYABLE ASPECTS OF BOAT-OWNING
come a few mandatory duties that, since they are inevitable, we
have decided to enjoy as well. After our Bahamian keel damage, we
schedule for a haul-out when we return to our home dock. The yard
crew slowly hoists *Velella*, cradled in an enormous sling, from her
favored medium to sit among the other displaced vessels in the dry
and sandy boatyard. Like a museum leviathan, propped up by wires
and braces, she stands, lifeless but majestic in the immensity of her
broad hull and full keel.

With a blast of pressurized water, we displace the organisms who,
in spite of inhospitable antifouling paint, have somehow managed to
gain foothold on *Velella*'s slick skin. Millions of miniscule skeleton
shrimp are swept away by the current of freshwater that we aim at
Velella's hull, their tiny claws still gripping tenaciously to strands of
algae or plantlike animals that we dislodge, and their skinny bodies
waving rapidly back and forth, gesticulating as if in desperate prayer,
as they die from the water's force and lack of essential salt. If only
these cling-ons had loosened their grip as *Velella* emerged from the
ocean, they would be safely floating now in the river instead of ac-
cumulating in windrows of desiccating exoskeletons upon the damp

sand, but a skeleton shrimp knows only to cling, whatever the consequences. In the myriad ancestors of these dying, clinging skeleton
shrimp, none could have anticipated such a profound environmental
change: first ripped from their comfortable habitat, exposed to the
dangerous dryness of air, then overwhelmed by the powerful current of freshwater. The success of skeleton shrimp results partly from
their blind reliance on a secure foothold, but that same steadfast grip
in the face of drastic change dooms these conformists to their fate. It
is difficult to come to grips with change, no doubt. Perhaps, like us,
there are a few skeleton shrimp who depart from the conservative
multitude's propensity to cling and so escape their unfortunate fate.
Those radical few might now be safe in the sea, vanguards of a new
future of skeleton shrimps in a world of change.

In addition to *Velella*'s normal reconditioning and necessary
keel repair, she needs several upgrades, and we are determined to
complete those jobs ourselves. We will repaint her topsides, the
white paint dull and chipped from twenty years of exposure to sun
and salt. We also plan to remove the white, flaking paint from her
wooden mast in order expose and varnish its wood. The longer she
sits in the yard, the drier her keel will become, and the final two tasks
on the list are keel repair and bottom paint.

We view the long hours ahead as investments, both in ourselves
and in *Velella*. We arise at dawn and work until dusk. Both the topsides and mast upgrades require extensive preparation before the
new layers of paint or varnish can be applied. We spend most of
one morning wiping down every centimeter of the topsides with
a strong solvent in order to remove any traces of wax, grease, and
grime, then perhaps another hour spraying the entire boatyard
with water to prevent the clouds of dust that follow each incoming,
wheeled vehicle from covering our just-cleaned boat. Ed repairs and
smoothes to perfection every small nick in the gel-coat, and I follow
with another thorough wipe with the solvent to ensure all traces of
dust are eliminated.

The yard crew is aghast when, instead of hiring the local epoxy guru with associated air-tank applicator, we use brushes to apply the polyurethane topsides paint ourselves, but by week's end we have gathered quite a following of like-minded, self-reliant souls. As layer after layer of gel-coat, undercoat, primary paint coat, and final paint coat replace each other, more and more people stop by our location in the yard to examine our progress. The final appearance of the new paint is beautiful, although the epoxy expert found a few brush-strokes. To us they are natural reminders of paint applied lovingly by hand. As I perch on the top rung of a stepladder and complete the paint job by applying *Velella*'s name and homeport using paint, brushes, and a penciled outline of the lettering, many an appreciative boater stops by to compliment us on our energy and determination. In perhaps the highest compliment, we begin to be consulted about the topsides of other boats—whether they needed new paint, gel-coat repair, or just a good buffing.

We never regret performing *Velella*'s maintenance ourselves. While in the yard, we take the time to go over her inch by inch. We become intimately acquainted with every system on our boat because our fingers and eyes touch each inch, from the lowest point on the keel to the mast-top. Ed repairs faulty wiring while I check all the through-hulls and dislodge debris that is partially clogging a scupper. By working on the boat ourselves, we come to know it, and can anticipate where the next repair is likely to be needed. The better we understand *Velella*, the easier it is for us to see her strengths and weaknesses. Because the repairs are our own, we are sure that they are done exactly as we want, with no shortcuts to haunt us later.

Moreover, the work itself is a chance to learn something new. Ed's explorations into 12-volt power systems and energy sources have resulted in freedom from electrical cables and companies, whether at the boat dock or in our mountain cabin. In addition, Ed has become an excellent diesel mechanic and can now practically disassemble and reassemble the engine himself. After our recent experiences with engine failures at most inopportune moments, we have learned to listen to the engine and to check on the amount of outflow from the cooling system.

While in the yard, we ask questions of the professional mechanics who are working on other boats, and they respond to us as equals. When Ed describes the repairs he made while we were cruising and relates how the engine was running above normal, the mechanic to whom he is speaking tells him that a warmer-than-normal engine probably means that the heat exchanger is due for cleaning. Since he happened to be flushing out one on another boat, he invites Ed to watch the operation and learn the procedure. After the tutorial, Ed returns to *Velella*, flushes the heat exchanger as he'd been taught, and blows out so much crud that we feel sure the problem is solved. When we return her to the water and can once again run the engine, it no longer overheats.

In one of our proudest moments of self-done repairs, which came later in our passages, we were able to identify and solve a problem that could have caused some serious damage. After a day of sailing in the nearby bay, we headed back up the river to our homeport against a strong current. The wind dropped off and we were soon losing ground to the falling tide. Since we wanted to be back in port before dark, we began to motor in. Something sounded different, and the engine's temperature rapidly shot up. I checked over the side and sure enough, no water was coming out of the exhaust from the raw-water cooling system. Quickly we moved to cut the engine and drop the hook, then Ed went below to examine the engine. Within a few minutes, he found that the raw-water impeller was not turning because it wasn't engaged to the shaft. After years of service, the shaft-impeller connection had just worn out. Ed needed a thin piece of metal for the repair, but we had no access to a machine shop where we could buy what we needed. Inspiration hit, and I volunteered my services by drinking the contents of a can of beer while Ed worked with the can itself. After cutting out a small piece and fitting it between the impeller and shaft, the raw-water system began to pump water again. Up came the anchor, the engine temperature remained normal, and we were back in port within an hour.

During this first season of boating and our first long cruise, we learned a lot about boats and about ourselves along the way. My confidence grew steadily as I learned to navigate—to plan our course, use the equipment, predict our arrival point and time, and read the charts and buoys correctly. I can handle sails that seemed immense on our first sail together and am proud of the repair I made to the mainsail while at sea. I've become adept, too, at steering and even traversing those dreaded inlets. I can make some repairs, although Ed is by far a better and more knowledgeable mechanic. Each of us can do everything that is needed, but each of us has areas of particular skill and expertise. All of it we learned by doing.

By sailing, we have discovered, too, that we are content to be alone with each other, immersed in nature and our surroundings. After this sailing cruise, we know that we can spend several days sailing together, restricted to a tiny living space, and feel closer because of the experience. Like any other couple, when tired and under stress we may argue, but more often, we stay on an even keel, discuss issues, and reach a consensus. We've learned that everyone on board must agree before we head offshore or even leave the dock; when a storm threatens, we must make decisions that are best for us all. Forced to rely on each other and to trust each other, the relationship either becomes stronger or falls apart.

We also both enjoy working—performing a job well and doing what needs to be done even if it would be easier to ignore the problem. Working on *Velella* makes it easy for us, however, for her beauty and performance reward a job that has been well done. While moving toward a goal, we take pleasure in the path we travel, defined as "work" to many people. What is the point of going to "work" so that you can be "free" to do something else? You are never free unless you are doing something that you want to do; even then, you are bound to others and bound by your own experiences. Freedom is an illusion and so is bondage. We knowingly and freely choose to bind ourselves to this boat by working on it. Are we free or bound? Both. Neither.

After repainting the topsides, we set to work on the mast. Before hauling-out, we unstepped her wooden but white-painted mast in order to recondition it, and it now rests on sawhorses beside us in the boatyard. Shorn of her mast and rigging, *Velella* reminds me of an elegant bird whose wings have been damaged so that it cannot fly. But *Velella*'s reconditioned wings will be replaced, and she will fly again. With gallons of paint stripper and a dozen sanding belts, we attack the chalky, flaking paint of the mast and expose the beautiful, golden spruce beneath. Within a week, we have transformed the mast from a big white stick piercing the center of our boat into a sailing mast that unifies the whole vessel. With its coatings of epoxy overlain by a dozen or more coats of varnish, the mast shines like glass, and we set to work immediately on the rest of the wood. A few more days, and the teak bulwarks, booms, bowsprit, wheel, blocks, gallows, hatches, boarding ladder, and cabin trim also gleam with their new layers of varnish.

While I apply additional coats of varnish, Ed attends to the messy keel repair. He soaks layers of woven fiberglass in epoxy resin and carefully applies them to the wounded hull. It is a giant, permanent Band-Aid. Once it is completely dry, he sands the patch smooth and covers it with bottom paint along with the rest of the hull. After almost two weeks in the yard, we are ready to go back in the water.

Again the giant cradle of slings is attached to *Velella* and she is carefully lifted up from the blocks and braces of jack stands supporting her. Once she is suspended in the slings, we paint the areas on the bottom of the keel that supported her while she rested on the ground. The yard crew gives us enough time to ensure that we are satisfied with the complete job before they maneuver the cradle and carefully lower *Velella* to float in the sea once again.

Restepping the mast is a delicate job. Ed built and varnished new fir spreaders, the cross-trees that hold the wire shrouds away from the mast, to replace the original ones in which we discovered rotten wood. The shrouds run from the top of the mast to the port and star-board sides of the boat, a backstay goes to the stern, and a forestay runs out to the tip of the bowsprit. All of this hardware was removed from the mast prior to our work on it and has been reconnected to the mast-top, polished, and inspected. A forklift, carefully maneu-vered by the best yard man around, supports the mast's weight as the rest of the yard crew and some interested boaters help to handle various lines and portions of the rigging. With *Velella* tightly tied off to the dock at low tide, the forklift eases with its precious cargo to the edge of a loading platform that overhangs the water. Slowly, the mast is lowered over the mast-step and we push it into place. I attach the backstay while Ed connects the forestay, then we each move to a port and starboard shroud. Once we have attached all the points, we disconnect the mast from the forklift and leisurely adjust the rigging.

Suddenly, *Velella* is whole again. Even the detractors who clung to the idea that a painted mast is easier to care for admitted that the varnished mast so improves *Velella's* appearance that our efforts are justified. Any brushstrokes in her new topsides paint are no longer noticeable as *Velella* floats in her medium. A bi-yearly trip up the mast to add a coat of varnish means that a regular examination of the mast's hardware is assured, but perhaps the greatest advantage is that we can see evidence of rot before we suffer the effects of a rotten spreader or mast base.

One day, when our work ends a little early because we are wait-ing for paint to dry, I try my hand at fishing. We take our dinghy out on the river, to a point where a small creek enters and a long-dead wax myrtle shrub has fallen into the water. On my first cast, I catch a beautiful little red drum, a fish I grew up calling a spot-tailed bass. It is coppery red in color with two uneven black spots where the tail fin joins the body. It is about a foot in length, perfectly pan sized, but too small to keep legally. Red drum have been so overfished that they have a small window of "keeper" sizes. The largest fish, which are the breeders, must be released, and the smallest fish, which are the juveniles, also must be released. I catch almost a dozen of the fish, but all are less than eighteen inches, which is the minimum size for keeping. It is disappointing to think that we hook not a single adult fish, but I hope that all the juveniles indicate that next season will be a strong one for the fish. We pull in our lines and decide to switch to shrimping. Thankfully, shrimp are abundant. Ed steers the dinghy along the shoreline of the creek while I toss the cast net. Every cast catches several shrimp, an occasional crab, and one small flounder. We take turns casting or steering until we have enough shrimp for supper. One of our friends on the docks says that crabs are as common as palmetto bugs and shrimp are the mosquitoes of the sea. He may be right; both crab and shrimp harvests have remained stable over the years.

When the English first arrived on the coast of North Carolina around 1585, the artist John White drew some of the animals they saw. He has a picture of a red drum, which is labeled as being five or six feet in length, the same size as striped bass. Sturgeon were common and were between ten and thirteen feet in length. While drum and striped bass still reach a large size, four feet is now about maximum for both species. Both species were severely overfished and affected by water pollution, but because of strict harvest regulations and restocking efforts, both species are recovering their numbers. Sturgeon, unfortunately, have not fared as well. They remain so rare that they are endangered. Long-lived and slow to reach maturity, the species will take a long time to recover, if it ever does.

As we float in the dinghy, a marsh hawk, or northern harrier, comes sweeping over the marsh on long, dark wings, a white patch glinting where the tail joins the body. It flies just above the tops of the tallest grasses, gliding easily on its outstretched wings, almost touching marsh grass. Suddenly, it hovers, head peering straight down, and dives. When it comes back up, it is carrying a marsh rat. Strong wing beats propel it away from the marsh toward the tree line, where we can no longer see it.

During our stay in the yard, we often walk around in the evenings just to enjoy the serenity of the deserted yard, after all the busy mechanics, crew, and owners have retired for the day, and we examine the other boats at the dock. One evening, a boat attracts our attention. At first glance, she seems to be another worn-out hulk, permanently tied to a dock for a few years until passing into oblivion. A closer look reveals that she was not damaged from neglect, but from hard use. The next day, we ask around and uncover the boat's story. Her current owners had bought her, moved aboard, and decided to head offshore for a yearlong cruise of the Caribbean. Three days out, they ran into a squall. The mast came down, punching holes in the cabintop and devastating the equipment on deck. Luckily, no damage was done below the waterline or to people aboard, and they were able to claw their way back inshore after a terrifying few days.

What her owners failed to realize, or chose to ignore, was rot in the white-painted wooden mast. Although the damage was present, a fresh coat of paint covered up the warning signs. One of the reasons that we removed our paint was in order to see the true status of the mast step and spreaders. In fact, we hadn't realized that our spreaders needed replacing until we stripped off the white paint and saw the blackened, softened wood underneath. Whitewash covers a multitude of sins.

During our long and dusty stay in the yard, we always appreciate the day's end. After a hard day of labor, we put away our tools and cans of paint or varnish, clean up our work area, and enjoy the tranquility of the peaceful yard. Surrounded on three sides by woodlands and facing the salt marsh and river, the evening attracts wildlife never even imagined in the bustling daytime. A local raccoon scours the grounds for the forgotten, half-eaten sandwich left by a hurried engine repairman, a bag of peanuts that spilled out as a painter opened it, or a can of soda overturned as a workman backed away to inspect his work. This particular raccoon had learned to check around the bases of boats, too, and was rewarded with a plentiful meal of skeleton shrimp, crabs, barnacles, and assorted other treats whenever a newly hauled boat was pulled from the river and stored in the yard. A stately great blue heron stalks through the yard and competes with the raccoon for the detritus removed from boat bottoms. It checks the docks, too, where fishermen and shrimpers have cleaned their catch and dropped a few shrimp heads or fish innards along the dock's edge.

Flocks of tree swallows and boat-tailed grackles dart in each evening before dusk to snatch a few mouthfuls of freshwater from the slowly dripping faucet of the pressure-washing machine, and several evenings a brilliantly colored painted bunting visits us. The multicolored bird alights in the lower branches of a magnificent live oak tree and waits patiently for the commoner birds to finish their activities, then he descends to a shallow pool of freshwater that has collected in a depression near the faucet. After a long and thorough bath, during which he splashes most of the water out of the pool, the bird returns to his perch and carefully preens each beautiful feather. He almost seems aware of his own beauty as he finishes his toilette, moving slowly and carefully for such a small bird, making sure each brightly colored blue, green, or red feather is in place and displayed to best effect.

Sadly, the number of painted buntings is declining significantly. Not only are they losing coastal breeding habitat to development, but as many as 80 percent of the nests of some populations are parasitized by brown cowbirds. Cowbirds lay their large eggs in bunting nests, and when the cowbird nestlings hatch, they are already larger and louder than their smaller nestmates. They outcompete, and in some cases physically remove, the other nestlings. The coup de grâce may come from their very beauty, as thousands are captured on their wintering grounds in Mexico and shipped to Europe in the pet trade.

After the creatures slow their wanderings, we pack up our gear and head to the shower rooms for a deserved, and necessary, shower. Even in the heat of summer, a hot shower on aching muscles at the end of the day is rejuvenating. We linger under hot water until our skin is as pink as cooked shrimp, duck briefly under cool water, then dry off, dress lightly, and head back outside. If we time it right, we walk out to the dock with a glass of cool wine or ice-cold beer and find a pleasant spot on the westernmost finger of the marina. There we lean our tired bodies against a piling and watch the sun drop below the river's surface, swallowed up by the water. A gentle breeze almost always springs up just before the sun departs, and draining our glasses, we walk back to the deserted yard hand in hand as the coolness of dusk descends, pleased with our day's work and the progress we have made. We can rest, satisfied in the knowledge that the time and effort we have invested results in a job done correctly, completely, and beautifully.

We are glad to finish our work in the yard and return to the sea. Just as the Sirens called to Ulysses from an island, the siren songs of our world come from the land as well. The songs of the ocean are songs of nature, many individual songs united into one harmony, but the terrestrial siren songs, at least nowadays, are chiefly songs of the individual alone, of greed and fleeting desires that create an appetite for needless things. They beckon us as sweetly to our destruction as Ulysses's Sirens called to him, but like him, binding ourselves securely to the mast of nature might allow us to escape their lure.

Moorings

AT DEAD LOW TIDE, WE EDGE *VELELLA* OUT OF THE MAIN RIVER channel and into a deep tidal creek. Creeping carefully along, we constantly evaluate our distance between its muddy banks. A single marker to starboard warns of an extensive sandy shoal that juts out to guard the mouth of the creek, and we sigh with relief once we safely glide past its nest of osprey chicks. Ahead lies *Velella*'s new home, a red mooring buoy floating in the placid creek. Beyond its mouth, the creek deepens and widens, and we focus our attention on the position of the buoy. A slight current is against us, and we see the smaller float and pick-up line trailing back toward us. Slowly we approach the buoy, and with a deft dip of the boot-hook, I have the pick-up line in hand. In a moment, it is around a cleat, and *Velella* comes to rest. Out first attempt to pick up a mooring is a success!

Learning to sail in the strong currents of the Southeast taught us to respect the power of unidirectional water flow. After that very first experience in docking crosscurrent, we've realized that instead of fighting it, the current can help us if we understand and utilize its force and motion. Water moving over the rudder gives us maneuverability, and by facing into the flow we achieve maximum maneuverability with minimum speed, a desirable combination for a heavy sailboat that does nothing quickly.

Once, while hauled-out in the boatyard, we saw the effects of underestimating the current. We were down on the docks when a sailboat came in, moving along with the tide instead of against it, mistaking its strength and their boat speed. Misjudging the turn into the slip and the force of water flow, the sailboat was T-boned on the end of a finger-dock as it hit with a report like a gunshot, the hull buckling inward into a sickening dent. There they remained, pinned like an insect, until the tide went slack and the current's force eased.

Our initial attachment to the mooring with the pick-up line is only temporary. We secure *Velella* for our absence by clipping her directly to the mooring at a U-bolt that passes through her hull at the bow just above the waterline. We loosen the pick-up line, but leave it attached as an added measure of safety. Then all is done and she is secure. We toss the six former docking lines into the dinghy along with all the rubber fenders, useless to us now, and head to a nearby dock. We have made arrangements with the dock owner to stow our dinghy and a dock-box ashore, and have, in fact, rented the mooring from him.

Although a mooring may not be unusual for sailboats in the Northeast, they are a little less common for southeasterners. Moorings require more organization in that gear as well as passengers are first stowed in the dinghy before being taken aboard, and water must be hauled out from the main dock in five-gallon cans, but those slight inconveniences are made up for by all the benefits.

Once aboard *Velella*, we revel in our freedom. No noisy generators running, no dock lights shining through the night, no curious visitors peering through the portholes—just the sound of the wind through the rigging and the wavelets against the hull. We are free, too, from the mats of spartina that become pinned between the dock and boat hull, and to which masses of scummy foam and a myriad of biting flies are attracted.

If truth be told, however, I do miss those masses of dead spartina.

Even more than in life, dead stalks of marsh grass support a diversity of animals, and I often lie down on the dock to peer into the water surrounding a spartina mat as if looking into an aquarium. In addition to the unpleasant hordes of biting flies, golden-winged, red-bodied dragonflies whose bulging eyes shine like rubies perch on the tips of upward-pointing sticks, darting out occasionally to catch a smaller fly. Interesting small fishes use the spartina mat as protection from predatory birds, camouflage from their larger, hungry cousins, and a food source. Tiny brown filefishes, each with a little spike erected on its head, move like hummingbirds as easily backward as forward. Equally small, boxy, yellow puffer fish, bodies covered in stiff spines that are only erect when the fish is frightened, move like small, motorized balloons among the filefish and spartina. The miniature fish carefully pick off bits of edible animals from spartina blades with their round mouths, and their eyes move independently like a chameleon's as they search for their prey.

Hanging from the undersides of branches, submerged in the water below, are animals whose rapid life cycle means that they can attach, grow, and reproduce before the spartina finally rots away and sinks. These include familiar barnacles as well as the less familiar, mossy bryozoans and hydrozoans, known locally as "grass," as in, "your boat hull is covered in grass." The dead blades and branches of spartina are covered with tiny green spheres of a colony of sea squirts, who are connected to each other by slender green cords of tissue through which blood ebbs and flows, like an umbilical cord. Each sphere is genetically identical to the other spheres, all produced by the single larval animal that first landed there. Are these spheres one individual or many? Because we are spatially distinct individuals, imagining colonial life is usually a stretch for our minds. It is easy to forget about the invisible cords that bind us to each other and to our environment as surely as those green cords of the sea squirt.

The view from the bow is of extensive expanses of salt marsh and tidal river, human activities only sporadically encroaching on river and marsh. The river's water is dark, its color provided by the extracted leaves and soil that have traveled from distant lands upstream. These nutrients, provided by the land and the river, nourish hordes of creatures. Blue crabs, oysters, and marsh grass live along the banks of river and creek, here where the river becomes one with the sea. Instead of boats, boat owners, and marina personnel, our neighbors are dolphins, birds, and an occasional fisherman who pulls into the sheltered creek.

Our noisiest visitors are boat-tailed grackles; although the brownish-colored females cackle frequently, it is the glossy-black males, feathers flashing in hues of the rainbow as sunlight splashes on them, that create a raucous, sometimes deafening noise as they perch in the rigging, each landing a step higher than the last. Like noisy humans jostling for the best seats in the stadium, they nudge and prod and shoulder each other aside, all the while cackling and fussing until even the best position here is not as good as the perch elsewhere, and off they fly en masse, to a tree across the creek, where their noisy din is lessened by distance.

At night, we are sometimes serenaded by the rhythmic grunts of croakers and other fishes that gather below our hull. The chorus comes from bow and stern, port and starboard sides; it is impossible to localize. Like katydids in treetops or tree frogs gathered around the edges of a summer pond, they call and respond in unison, one starting the chorus, then dozens of voices joining in, and always to a methodical rhythm of some hymn only they recognize.

Sometimes we also hear the startled pops of snapping shrimp as they react to a close encounter with one of the fish, or an unwelcome visit from another shrimp neighbor. The small shrimp live in the tangle of animals that grows on the boat hull and dock, and we also find them hidden among the oysters during low tide. They cock open one large claw, and when disturbed, the resounding "pop" as it abruptly snaps closed is loud enough to hear through the boat hull at night or from many feet away on the mudbank.

After arriving on our mooring and relaxing a bit, we are surprised to see a familiar boat tied up to a small dock almost exactly opposite us, on the other side of the creek. Just before our trip south, while tied up to a marina in Beaufort, this boat docked behind us. We met her owners, and they related their harrowing experience of bringing her down the ICW from not more than a couple of hundred miles north. With neither sails nor engine functional, they were towed nearly the whole way, and with a deep-drafted, heavy boat, the trip was less than enjoyable. They bought the boat after falling in love and dreaming of adventures together, but each had a different idea of what the adventure should entail. Neither of them had an inkling of the amount of work required before the boat was safe even to leave at the dock, much less to take for a sail.

The boat's first owner had been a master carver, and she was decorated with some magnificent woodwork both above and below decks. For her new owners those beautiful accents masked a multitude of defects. To begin with, she was built of ferrocement—a strong material, no doubt, and one that has supporters, but to us cement is the very last material that seems appropriate for a boat. All her standing rigging was heavily rusted, running rigging was nonexistent, and her sails were only slightly more substantial than paper napkins. Both masts were wooden, painted, and suspect, and somewhere there was a leak bad enough to keep the bilge pump in near-constant use. Her new owners faced an enormous task in bringing the boat back into serviceable condition.

It had been a few months since we'd seen them, and we wondered how they were doing. The boat didn't look significantly different, even though Velella's appearance and our experiences had changed drastically in the same amount of time. We later learned that just as the owners had begun to make a little headway, they split up, their dreams of adventure and each other no longer enough to sustain them. The boat was moved to the small, out-of-the-way dock, and now, floating rather pitifully across the creek, she seemed abandoned to her fate, a symbol of dreams defeated by reality, and of individuals failing to find common ground.

With our freedom from the inconveniences of land came the freedom from that ever-present, snakelike, yellow umbilicus connecting our boat to land-based power supply. Ed estimated our daily power consumption as we prepared to cut *Velella's* tie to land and replaced shore power with an appropriately sized solar panel and wind generator. We considered that alone, neither could be relied upon for a near-constant power source in our location, but for the most part, either the sun shone or the wind blew most of the time. Although both required an initial outlay for their purchase, the cost difference between marina slip rates and a mooring paid for both the solar and wind generators within three months. The addition of a durable improvement not only liberated us from dockside power, but also upgraded *Velella* for long-distance cruising. So often, it is easy to overlook the long-term gains when a short-term investment is required. The failure to recognize long-term gain over short-term expense is a fundamental difficulty that prevents improvements at all levels of our society and personal lives.

Instead of relying on energy generated solely by the consumption of fossil fuels, we rely on the renewable resources of sunlight and wind. Just by unplugging from the "grid," we contribute a little to the longevity of those finite resources and have a small but real effect on retaining some of the quality of our environment. As we lie awake reading books after dark, it is pleasurable to consider that we are reading by the light of wind and sun. No longer does the wind provide us only with a medium for travel, but it also allows us to read after dark, to operate equipment, and even to make ice! I never realized how energy-expensive it is to freeze water until we had to generate our own power to heat water to boiling or freeze it into ice. Ice is a luxury—often unnecessary, expensive to make—that is consumed largely without thought. At the end of a long, hot day, a glass of liquid with ice in it is welcome on our boat, but our pleasure is enhanced because we appreciate that it is an extravagance and treat it as such.

Our experiences in sailing through the salt marshes and offshore, the self-reliance we came to feel, and the independence that we enjoyed all combined to make us consider a mooring over a marina. We were looking for others who were trying to escape from a humdrum life, become immersed in a creative lifestyle, or just experience the simple pleasure of skimming about the ocean's and river's surface. We longed to find some others, like ourselves, who enjoyed taking their boats out for whatever few hours they could spare in hopes of experiencing something different from the norm.

After attaching to our mooring in the quiet little creek, we began to meet the local people who frequented the nearby docks, and grew to appreciate them with each visit. Like us, they are escaping the boredom and preoccupation with a mediocre life driven by consumption and comparison, and every one of them seems to feel at home and most alive while on the water. One old codger who could barely get his small johnboat unloaded from his trailer at the nearby boat ramp came to life the moment he cranked up the motor: his back straightened, his feeble hands suddenly became strong as visegrips, and a slight smile lifted the corners of his weary mouth. Hours would pass before he returned from zipping about the many waterways, apparently completely rejuvenated.

The dock's owner, The Captain, is one of the more interesting people we have met. A straight-talking, no-nonsense, almost gruff fellow, he is also as warmhearted and helpful as a saint. We heard about his small dock by word of mouth, although we had seen it from the river and wondered about it before. When he suggested his only mooring to us at a reasonable rate, we were elated and began to make plans for our move. He warned us that we should consider dropping an anchor as a backup to the mooring and that we ought to inspect all the components before attaching. We tied up to his dock for a few weeks in late summer while examining the mooring and traveling back to our land-based home, and by the time we arrived in September, ready for the move, were surprised to see a bright new buoy replacing the old faded one. As he explained it, the local floating crane just happened by his dock one day to do some work across the creek, and he contracted with them to sink a completely new, several-times-upgraded mooring. We figure this one might survive a hurricane, although we hope never to test it.

Another interesting couple is the pair of sole live-aboards on the dock who have a beautiful, wooden, 1930s-built schooner. The boat is a big job to care for, but they manage to keep her in reasonably good condition. While his wife spends countless hours working at her land-based job, Alex shrimps. He is a friendly, enthusiastic fellow and tries hard, but bad luck seems to follow him like a stray dog. Each time we arrive at the dock, we hear of some recent experience and commiserate with him over his misfortune. The Captain summed it up one day by observing that one day soon, poor Alex would have a good day shrimping—it's just the law of averages, he said, that out of all those days spent on the water, Alex would have good luck at least once. Alex never gives up, his enthusiasm never wavering, and every day during the summer and fall seasons he is up at dawn to try his luck again.

While his wife continues to count out Alex's entire haul of that day's shrimp into a couple of one-pound bags, Alex stops to tell us of his latest misadventures aboard his tiny shrimp boat. Just yesterday he entangled the shrimp net in the boat's propeller so that he had to dive in and cut the propeller free while drifting out to sea; last week his second net was fouled on the bottom and torn into pieces; he has even had a net and entire rig somehow come loose from the boat during one drag, then spent another day or two retrieving it; and he has dragged up dozens of crab pots that defeat the net by allowing the shrimp to escape. So many people seem to grow tired and depressed from any misfortune, refusing to appreciate the joys that life offers. For Alex, however, a little salt spray in the air and a few shrimp in the cooler are enough to satisfy him. He counts every difficulty as another great adventure as well as a good story, and appreciates every day for whatever it offers.

While admiring a new and undamaged pot that Alex has set aside to sell, I learn quite a bit about commercial crabbing. The "pots" are big, square cages that are made from very heavy-duty, plastic-coated chicken wire. They are almost identical to those from the Chesapeake Bay, described by William Warner in *Beautiful Swimmers*, his classic book of blue crabs and crabbing. The bottom of the cage is framed around all four sides by heavy rebar that prevents the pot from tumbling in swift river currents. Around the middle of the pot are four openings, one to a side, which allow the crabs to enter. They are short funnels, more narrow toward the inside of the trap, and although the crabs can force their way in through them, they are usually unable to orient their bodies correctly to make their way back out. The bait-well is in the center of the trap, toward the bottom rather than the top, and this particular pot was ingeniously designed by using a piece of lightweight bungee cord to hold the hinged bait door closed. The crabber who worked pots like this one could simply flip the pot upside down, pull on the bait door, load the bait-well, then allow the bungee cord to pull it tight. A section of chicken wire called the apron divides the upper and lower halves of the cage, with an opening in its center providing a passageway between the two compartments. By dividing the cage into two parts, the apron provides more corners for crabs to collect in, gives smaller crabs a place to escape larger, more aggressive ones, and it allows crabs to move away from the bait after feeding so they are not constantly in competition with the newly arrived, hungry crabs who are ready to defend the source of food they have just discovered. At the upper corners of the cage, small holes allow the smallest crabs to escape outside the trap and grow larger in the river until they reach harvestable size. It has been said that in some places, the crab pots are so abundant that they should be considered a means of culturing crabs: instead of foraging for food in the wild, the small crabs rely instead on cage food and move from pot to pot until they finally get too big to escape.

Another of the crab traps that Alex has unintentionally caught in his net has been subtly vandalized so that it will not catch crabs. The four doors that allow the crabs to enter have been just barely pushed closed. A quick glance at the trap shows nothing out of the ordinary, and the doors can be easily opened up again if their closure was noticed. According to the locals, this type of vandalism is used when a newcomer drops his pots in the established territory of another crabber. The vandalized newcomer would pull his pots, find no crabs in them, assume they were in a poor location, and move on to another area. By this subterfuge, confrontation was usually avoided and the newcomer moved from place to place until he discovered what was wrong with his traps and set them in an uncontested location.

An older, less well-constructed crab pot is also perched among the items collected during Alex's trawling operations. This one is extensively bent, crushed and cut in places so completely that it appears as if an angry crabber used heavy pliers and a crowbar, or else the trap must have been crushed in Alex's rig as he hoisted it aboard. The damage is too extensive for a bare-handed human to have caused. I am utterly surprised when The Captain says nonchalantly that a loggerhead sea turtle is the culprit. He tells me that they use their bills with incredible force, crushing and in places actually biting through the metal, to get at the crabs inside. I thought that turtles ate jellies, and the turtles themselves are such placid creatures that it is hard for me to imagine a loggerhead turtle as a giant can-opener. After checking the library, however, I discovered that many sea turtles do, indeed, eat crabs as well as jellies.

One reason that sea turtles arouse the emotions of people who love or hate them is their symbolism of free nature brought to the brink of extinction by humans. First we collected their eggs so efficiently that we compromised their normal cycle of producing enough offspring to reach adulthood. Just as efficiently, we also collected the adults both directly from the sea and as they came ashore to lay eggs, turning them into turtle-shell hairpins or soup. Uncountable numbers were killed by drowning in fishing nets; now nets on trawling boats, especially the shrimpers in our waters, must have turtle-excluding devices. The plastic bags that we dump offshore are sometimes mistaken for edible jellies by the turtles; they eat them, then die of a blocked intestine. Yet they swim out there in the open ocean, in a place over which we seem to have so little control, and they've been doing so for millions of years. When the first human gingerly set out upon the surface of the sea, sea turtles were already an ancient tribe of seafarers. If nothing else, the dwindling numbers of turtles shows us just how far our reach can extend. We are confronted by the stark reality of this connection between our actions and their consequences.

There are a couple of crabbers who keep their clean, white boats rafted up together on one end of the dock. Each morning during crab season they load crates onto the afterdeck of their low, open boats and head out to check their pots. It is not unusual, at the height of the season, for them to bring in 7,000 pounds of crabs during one morning. Their boats are well-designed work boats, with a wide, clear workspace and low gunwales to make easy work of lifting the pots up and over the sides. Each has a rigid canopy that protects the men and their catch from the intense summer sun but does not affect their speed as they race from pot to pot. They keep their boats scrupulously clean, even washing things down with Clorox on occasion.

With all this local knowledge, literally tons of crabs passing the docks, and a fellow such as The Captain to befriend us, it was inevitable that we would be introduced to a true-to-life version of Frogmore stew. Frogmore is an actual town, just a few miles from Beaufort, South Carolina, on the sea island road. There are many variations on Frogmore stew, but the "real" one, as defined by The Captain and his family, who, after all, should know what constitutes a real Frogmore stew, contains boiled sausage, corn-on-the-cob, crabs, and shrimp. The sausage was a special brand favored by The Captain, who kept his freezer stocked with it, the corn came from a local roadside stand, a bucketful of crabs was donated from among the thousands that came off the crab boats, but we were to supply the shrimp that evening.

Ed and I have done low-tech shrimping, just tossing our cast net along the shoreline at low tide from the dinghy, but The Captain promises to teach us how to catch the most and largest shrimp by using bait. The first task is to prepare the bait. As the lightest of the three, I am voted official baiter, and at low tide walk out into the soft mud at the edge of the marsh with a bait bucket full of dry fish meal and a rake. On the dock, The Captain tosses his cast net, and we take its landing point as the average throwing distance. Using a line of that length as a measuring device, he marks a spot on the dock with his end of the line, and I lay the fish meal bait at the other end. We mark out several sites this way as we move along the length of the dock, The Captain holding one end of the line and marking the spot on the dock while I sprinkle bait over an area about two feet square and rake it into the mud at the other end. By mixing the bait into the mud, we hope to keep it from washing away too quickly and the shrimp busy trying to separate food from mud.

After baiting the mudflat, I take the opportunity at low tide to poke around and examine the animals living there. The Captain was surprised that I so readily agreed to lay the bait, but I love stomping through the ankle-deep mud, turning over old shells and checking the shallows to see what has been exposed by the retreating tide. My own pleasure is reflected in a stanza from David Slavitt's poem "Day Sailing":

> The cove at low tide
> swarms, gulls and terns,
> sandpipers, and crows
> pick over the shingle,
> small crabs start,
> clams squirt, worms
> snake in the rich reek
> of sea-wrack rot.
> The muck smacks soles,
> oozes between my toes.

Usually, however, I carry a shovel and sieve onto a mudflat, instead of a rake. Much to The Captain's amusement, I reluctantly abandon the mudflat only after he agrees to show me how to make mud balls of shrimp bait.

Using a special type of very stiff, nearly dry mud that he had collected earlier, we scoop up a big ball of it from his bucket of mud and begin to work in the powdery bait, kneading the mud balls like bread dough until the mud begins to fall apart and will hold no more bait. We plan to use the balls to replenish the bait sites as they are exhausted, but we discover that the baited squares draw in plenty of shrimp and last longer than we do at shrimping.

At last, everything is prepared for shrimping, and we wait impatiently for the rising tide to cover the baited sites. High tide falls after dark, just about suppertime, which is perfect timing, from The Captain's point of view. We duly wait until sunset and meet him and his wife in the dockhouse to begin the evening's festivities.

Ed and I begin to toss the cast net toward the now-submerged baits, using the marks on the dock and a rough estimate of distance from the dock. We haul in several very large shrimp, exclaiming over their size, but The Captain observes that we will be waiting until midnight for supper if we catch shrimp at such a slow rate. We turn over the cast net, and like a man born to salt marshes and shrimp, The Captain loads the cooler after a single round at the baits. He returns to the dockhouse with shrimp while we continue to add a few more with each cast. We quickly become more interested in the preparation of supper, however, and give the startled shrimp that have escaped our clumsy throws some time to return to the baits.

The Captain's wife has already cooked the sausage and corn in a huge kettle of boiling, seasoned water, and put them into a small cooler so they will stay hot. On our arrival, the crabs are just coming out of the kettle, and The Captain and his wife set to work cleaning them. With dexterity developed from years of practice, they pop off the carapace, quickly remove the backfin and rinse it briefly, break off the two large claws, drop claws and backfin into the hot-cooler, and push the carapace and inedible organs into a central pile. In what seems like an instant, they have prepared a few dozen crabs and put the shrimp on to boil. The shrimp are cooked quickly, just long enough for them to turn pink and then a wee bit longer, then they are removed from the boiling water, added to the hot-cooler, and we head to the table for our feast.

We seat ourselves at a rickety old wooden table with newspapers for a placemat and a roll of paper towels for napkins. We pass around the coolers full of food and pile our plates with the fare. We take turns, every quarter hour or so, pushing back from the table, picking up our cast nets, and throwing a round—one toss at each bait, caught shrimp tossed into a large cooler, then back to the table while more shrimp move in to the bait. Now this is the way to shrimp!

We take turns, too, telling stories of our pasts. With huge piles of refuse from the crab and shrimp skeletons beside each of us, The Captain tells of his youth as a boy roaming the nearby creeks and rivers, and becoming adept at drawing enough from the strange mix of land and sea to provide for his family. Instead of greedily robbing the marsh of all it had to offer, he was content to make just enough to live comfortably. We listen intently, while with equal concentration, we extract the delicious bits of crab from the backfin, crack open the heavy claws, and peel the shrimp. We are relative novices at eating crabs compared to The Captain and his wife, but with some tips from those two seasoned veterans, we spend the delightful evening improving our technique.

Our shrimping improves, too, as we became familiar with the rhythm of throwing the net. The Captain's motions when casting are like a ballet, as he stands, silhouetted against the salt marsh by the rising moon, gracefully casting his net in a single easy motion, huge hands gently tugging on the line to retrieve the net from the sea. Like a mariner of ancient times, he draws his sustenance from the sea and understands its rhythms and those of the creatures it contains.

At last, our stomachs full and the coolers empty, we begin to tire. Shoulders aching from the unaccustomed motion, the accuracy of our casts begins to suffer. The early evening's breeze has picked up into a strong wind, and our minds begin to drift toward the dinghy ride back to *Velella*. It is time to go. We fold up the newspaper placemats and dump their loads of shrimp and crab carcasses over the dock's edge, back into the sea that had provided them to us, to feed the next generation of creatures on the remains.

Back aboard *Velella*, dinghy tied off safely beside us, we listen to the wind as it blows the surface of the creek into small wavelets that caress our sides. Only a slight, occasional tug reminds us of our attachment to the mooring. The gentle hum of the turbine as it charges the batteries brings a smile to my face as I cut off the reading lamp beside me. We sleep peacefully, knowing that we have found a good home for our boat and ourselves.

Reflections

It is a baking-hot day in September on the coast of South Carolina. Rhythmic stridulation of buzzing cicadas ebbs and flows from nearby live oaks while the sun beats down from a cloudless sky. By noon, the sunlight is so intense that the colors of the salt marsh appear faded, like the fabric of a favorite shirt whose shoulders have paled from deep green to the light yellow of old straw.

We left our mooring early to sail in the wide river, but the morning's wind ceased as the day progressed, and now we float quietly. The river's current is gentle, the tide having just turned, and we are peacefully pulled, ever so slightly, toward the sea. The air is so still that the wide river is perfectly calm, a sheet of glass; no waves disturb its surface. I stare into its depths and see myself staring back. Each line and sail is also reflected, another *Velella* there in the river. I could trace our lines and draw a perfect copy of our boat, paint it on the painted river just as Coleridge imagined:

> Day after day, day after day,
> We stuck, nor breath nor motion;
> As idle as a painted ship
> Upon a painted ocean.

A fish suddenly breaks the surface in the middle of my face; the ripples from its contact spread out from that central point to disturb the reflection and release me.

The afternoon's heat increases until *Velella's* decks are blistering, the teak so hot that we are unable to stand still on our bare feet. At last, the heat too intense for us, we launch ourselves overboard, into welcoming coolness of river. We float quietly in the river, drifting with its current, then swim to our docking ladder that hangs over *Velella's* side, where we pause before returning on deck. After only a few minutes on deck, the humid air is so thick and hot that it seems hard to breathe and so we return to the water.

We linger in the river until a zephyr disturbs the water's surface. Like a feather drawn across our cheeks, it tickles the hairs on our faces and the damp curls on the backs of our necks. Just a breath, but cool, more refreshing than ice cream on a summer day. We head up on deck again before *Velella* can sail away without us and watch as each new breath of air is made visible on the water.

But wait—a cool breeze after such a blistering day? We gaze upward, and there, on the horizon, is a black line of clouds growing taller and wider. Quickly, then, we move to take in sails, set the anchor, and double-cleat the dinghy. With everything secured, we move back on deck to await the coming storm.

The black clouds pile atop each other, each clambering over the back of another to reach the apex of the mound. Soon they obscure the sun, and a sickly-green, evening darkness settles in, even though it is only midafternoon. Up the river, we see the wind coming. Small waves, followed immediately by whitecaps, race toward us, and a huge gust of cold, wet wind rocks us on our side. The spartina in the marsh bends level with the water in which it stands, and big live oaks on a nearby island moan and complain as the wind tears through their branches. A single old palmetto tree loses one of its fronds, which goes whipping away through the air until it stops abruptly against the base of an oak.

Just behind the wind is the rain, in torrents. We see it too as it charges across the water toward us, like a gray sheet being pulled across the river. Now there is no distinction between the water in the sky and that of the river, just one liquid mass. We duck below, but leave one door of the companionway open to watch the drama.

Waves are rolling past us, and *Velella* sways over to her side with each gust of wind. The sound is deafening—of wind in our rigging, of dead limbs breaking from the old live oaks, of rain pounding like hailstones on our cabintop and the water's surface. We hear *Velella* strain against her anchor line with each gust as if she longs to be free to sail before the wind, using its power to her advantage.

The smell of the rain is distinctive, too. After the suffocating heat, the cool air seems full of salt marsh and sweetness. It so permeates the air that I can taste it on my lips when I lick them. Not the taste of pure salt, as comes from sweat or from the ocean, but a complex mixture. There is the most pleasant hint of old leaves and green moss, contributions from the land, coupled with the strong flavor of mud, salt water, and decaying spartina blades from the marsh. I can even smell the clean iodine aroma of a popping shrimp, the sharp ammonia odor of a tiny shark, or the near-absence of scent, certainly an absence of any "fishy" odor, from a living fish. That fragrance, of the southeastern salt marsh during a thunderstorm, is like no other scent I have ever encountered. If it could be bottled and then opened in front of a blindfolded person, I'm sure they could see an expanse of green spartina, murky water flowing past, snowy egrets fishing along the edges of an oyster bank.

The storm abates, its ferocity dwindling quickly away. Like a mayfly, its passion is intense but ephemeral. Only its aroma and a lingering coolness of the air remain as indications of its passage. We reemerge from *Velella*'s cabin onto her deck.

The salt marsh seems so constant, a predictable sea of green marsh grass and brown river water, identical to any other expanse of grass and water, but any one section of the marsh is constantly changing. The waves generated by this one thunderstorm have eaten away at that exposed bank, undercutting the nearby island ever more. With each tide, sediment is carried out of the inlet and deposited somewhere offshore, building a shoal in one location while another shoal is being swept out of existence. The next storm, from a different direction, might finally push the old leaning palmetto tree into the river, the bank underneath it succumbing to the hunger of the waves.

Change will come to the spartina blades, the river banks, the inlet's channel, even while the overall salt marsh, the river, and the ocean seem to stay the same. Neither do the smallest components, the sand grains and water drops, change their basic form. Those molecules of water flowing past right now are on their way to the sea. How long will they mix with the sea, be part of the ocean, until they are drawn up again into clouds, fall as rain in the Appalachian Mountains, percolate through the soil and tiny streams until they once again reach a river and travel back down to the sea? And to think that this minute amount, the small pool I hold in my cupped hand as I float here on my boat in this dark river, might have been to the depths of the ocean, been swallowed by a whale, brushed past the *Titanic*, maybe even been frozen in the iceberg that sank her, fallen as rain in the Amazonian rainforest, condensed as the dew sipped by a butterfly on its migration flight to Mexico, and slipped down the throat of a thirsty Native American before Europeans arrived on his shore. I could spend a lifetime contemplating the possible resting places of this handful of river water and snowflakes and dewdrops. Impossible to contain, it drips slowly from my fingertips and falls back into the river.

Some lingering droplets from the thunderstorm splash on the deck where I stand. Looking upward, I see more of them falling from the mast-top, descending toward my upturned face. I close my eyes as they strike me, warmed already by the sun's return, and as I open my eyes again to look at an oyster bank in the marsh, they blur my vision, and I see, instead, a Native village rising out of a nearby glade.

I am afloat here in this river of time. Here at the edge of the sea and the land, the river's current ebbs and flows, back and forth, a breath drawn in and out. This river is dark and deep, this river that so captivates my mind as well as my body. I catch snatches through my senses—the odor of the marsh, the taste of salty air, the pop of a shrimp, the form of an island, the cool seaward flow of water over skin—each a beautiful fragment that reveals itself not just as a part, but as the whole. When I close my eyes, my mind is set adrift in form and lost in time. The river outflows its banks to embrace the sea, clouds, rain, and fog, its flow transforms the land as its rich, black sediment transmutes into shrimp, fish, birds, and people of different appearances, histories, and cultures. In endless cycles of interbeing, all begins and ends in the river, and then beginnings and endings unite in one eternal moment. One last droplet falls from my fingertip into the river. As it enters, no longer is there an illusion of individuality. The droplet becomes the river again.

Acknowledgments

Individuals who read the entire manuscript and offered suggestions for improvement include an anonymous reviewer, Susan Cohen, Richard Fox, and Edward Ruppert. Suzanne Bell read an early draft. The staff of the Brevard College library, especially Brenda Spillman and Mike McCabe, assisted with locating reference materials. The staff of University Press of Florida, especially Sian Hunter, improved the overall quality of the book, and I have enjoyed working with them. Copy editor Susan Murray provided a careful and welcome review of the final manuscript.

The purpose of most of my coastal excursions to salt marshes, mudflats, and other marine habitats was to provide living animals for study by students, but as any teacher knows, teaching others is the best way of learning oneself. I thank Brevard College and Clemson University for their support of my teaching career and the many students in my courses for sharing their fascination for marine life with me. A yearlong postdoctoral fellowship at the Smithsonian Marine Station at Fort Pierce, Florida, was an enjoyable opportunity to learn even more about the biology of marine animals, and I thank the former director, Mary Rice, and her staff at the station for their encouragement.

I revised and edited this book during a sabbatical year from Brevard College and thank Brevard College and the Appalachian College Association for sabbatical support. Bland Simpson mentored and encouraged me during my recent and a previous sabbatical.

Both *Mountain Nature* and *Waterways* have benefited from his expertise.

So far, Ed and I have owned five sailboats, a 27-foot Ericson named *Asplanchna*, a 37-foot Tayana named *Velella*, a 34-foot Pacific Seacraft named *Skimmer*, a 38-foot Panda named *Water Bear*, and a 27-foot Nor'Sea named *Clio*. We enjoy the camaraderie of the sailing community and have made many friends who share our sense of adventure. We are pleased to now have a home at Sea Harbour Yacht Club in Oriental, North Carolina, managed by Paul Olson and the incomparable Lisa Thompson.

Although all the adventures related herein really occurred, the order of some events was changed and the names of everyone, other than Jennifer and Ed, are fictional.

References

Ammons, Archie Randolph. "Small Song." In *The Selected Poems 1951–1977*, 69. New York: Norton, 1977.

Atlantic Deeper Waterways Association. *The Atlantic Intra-coastal Waterway: The Project Advocated by the Atlantic Deeper Waterways Association. Official Survey Lines and Present Status of the Work in Its Various Sections*. Philadelphia, 1923. Reprint, Ulan Press, 2012.

Atlantic States Marine Fisheries Commission. *American Shad Stock Assessment Report for Peer Review*. Vols. 1–3. Atlantic States Marine Fisheries Commission, Stock Assessment Report No. 07-01, Supplement, 2007. www.asmfc.org/.

Bartram, William. *The Travels of William Bartram: Naturalist's Edition*. Edited by Francis Harper. Athens: University of Georgia Press, 1998.

Beebe, William. *Book of Bays*. New York: Harcourt, Brace, 1942.

Bentley, Matt, Peter Olive, and Kim Last. "Sexual Satellites, Moonlight and the Nuptial Dances of Worms: The Influence of the Moon on the Reproduction of Marine Animals." *Earth, Moon, and Planets* 85 (1999): 67–84.

Blazer, Vicki, Luke Iwanowicz, Deborah Iwanowicz, David Smith, J. A. Young, James Hedrick, S. W. Foster, and Stephen Reeser. "Intersex (Testicular Oocytes) in Smallmouth Bass from the Potomac River and Selected Nearby Drainages." *Journal of Aquatic Animal Health* 19 (2007): 242–53.

Bowne, Eric. *The Westo Indians: Slave Traders of the Early Colonial South*. Tuscaloosa: University of Alabama Press, 2005.

Brinnin, John Malcolm. "Skin Diving in the Virgins." In *One Hundred American Poems of the Twentieth Century*, edited by Laurence Perrine and James Reid, 238. New York: Harcourt, Brace, 1966.

Buffett, Jimmy. "Prince of Tides." From the album *Hot Water*. MCA Records, 1988.

Carson, Rachel. *The Edge of the Sea.* New York: Houghton Mifflin, 1955.
———. *The Sea around Us.* New York: Oxford University Press, 1951.
———. *Silent Spring.* New York: Houghton Mifflin, 1962.
Centers for Disease Control. *Fourth National Report on Human Exposure to Environmental Chemicals.* 2009.
Clark, Leonard Bertrand, and Walter Norton Hess. "Swarming of the Atlantic Palolo Worm *Leodice fucata.*" *Carnegie Publishing* 524 (1940): 21–27.
Clarke, Arthur C. "The Nine Billion Names of God." In *The Nine Billion Names of God: The Best Short Stories of Arthur C. Clarke.* New York: Signet, 1974.
Colborn, Theo, Dianne Dumanoski, and John Peter Myers. *Our Stolen Future.* New York: Penguin, 1996.
Coleridge, Samuel Taylor. "Eolian Harp." In *Coleridge Poetical Works,* 100–102. 1912. New York: Oxford University Press, 1973.
———. "Rime of the Ancient Mariner." In *Coleridge Poetical Works,* 186–209. 1912. New York: Oxford University Press, 1973.
Dana, Richard Henry. *Two Years before the Mast.* Reprint, New York: Signet Classics, 1964.
DeMent, Iris. "Easy's Gettin' Harder Every Day." From the album *My Life.* Warner Bros. Records, 1994.
Dykeman, Wilma. *The French Broad.* Newport, Tenn.: Wakestone, 1955.
Earle, Sylvia. *Sea Change: A Message of the Oceans.* New York: Fawcett, 1995.
Forester, Cecil Scott. *The Hornblower Saga.* 11 novels. Boston: Little, Brown, 1962.
Frankenberg, Dirk. *The Nature of North Carolina's Southern Coast: Barrier Islands, Coastal Waters, and Wetlands.* Chapel Hill: University of North Carolina Press, 1997.
Gallay, Alan. *The Indian Slave Trade.* New Haven: Yale University Press, 2002.
Garstang, Walter. "Conaria and Co." In *Larval Forms and Other Zoological Verses,* 29. Chicago: University of Chicago Press, 1985.
Glover, Lorri, and Daniel Blake Smith. *The Shipwreck That Saved Jamestown: The Sea Venture Castaways and the Fate of America.* New York: Holt, 2009.
Guillette, Louis, Timothy Gross, Greg Masson, John Matter, H. Franklin Percival, and Allan Woodward. "Developmental Abnormalities of the Gonad and Abnormal Sex Hormone Concentrations in Juvenile Alligators from Contaminated and Control Lakes in Florida." *Environmental Health Perspectives* 102 (1994): 680–88.

Hardy, Alister. *The Open Sea: Its Natural History.* Boston: Houghton Mifflin, 1965.

Harriot, Thomas. "A Brief and True Report of the New Found Land of Virginia (1588)." *Electronic Texts in American Studies,* Paper 20, edited by Paul Royster. http://digitalcommons.unl.edu/etas/20.

Hay, John. *The Way to the Salt Marsh: A John Hay Reader.* Edited by Christopher Merrill. Hanover, N.H.: University Press of New England, 1998.

Heath, Julie, Peter Frederick, James Kushlan, and Keith Bildstein. White Ibis (*Eudocimus albus*). In The Birds of North America Online, edited by A. Poole. Ithaca: Cornell Lab of Ornithology, 2009. http://bna.birds. cornell.edu/bna/species/009doi:10.2173/bna.9.

Joyce, Stephanie. "The Dead Zones: Oxygen-Starved Coastal Waters." *Environmental Health Perspectives* 108, no. 3 (2000): A120.

Klopchin, Jeanette, Jill Stewart, Laura Webster, and Paul Sandifer. "Assessment of Environmental Impacts of a Colony of Free-Ranging Rhesus Monkeys (*Macca mulatta*) on Morgan Island, South Carolina." *Environmental Monitoring and Assessment* 137 (2008): 301–13.

Lawson, John. *A New Voyage to Carolina.* Annotated ed. Chapel Hill: University of North Carolina Press, 1967.

Lopez, Thomas. *Ruby: Adventures of a Galactic Gumshoe.* Fort Edward, N.Y.: ZBS Foundation, 1982.

McPhee, John. *The Founding Fish.* New York: Farrar, Straus, and Giroux, 2002.

Melville, Herman. *Moby Dick.* Reprint, New York: Simon and Schuster, 1999.

Milling, Chapman James. *Red Carolinians.* 2nd ed. Chapel Hill: University of North Carolina Press, 1969.

Murphy, Robert Cushman. *Logbook for Grace.* New York: Macmillan, 1947.

Oliver, Mary. "Poem for the One World." In *A Thousand Mornings,* 15. New York: Penguin, 2012.

Parkman, Aubrey. *History of the Waterways of the Atlantic Coast of the United States.* National Waterways Study, U.S. Army Engineer Water Resources Support Center, Institute for Water Resources, 1983.

Penn Center. www.penncenter.com/.

Perry, Richard. *At the Turn of the Tide: A Book of Wild Birds.* New York: Taplinger, 1972.

Rembert, David. "The Carolina Plants of Andre Michaux." *Castanea* 44 (1979): 65–80.

Ruppert, Edward, and Richard Fox. *Seashore Animals of the Southeast: A Guide to Common Shallow-Water Invertebrates of the Southeastern Atlantic Coast.* Columbia: University of South Carolina Press, 1988.

Sagan, Carl. *Cosmos.* Ballantine, 1985.

Semenza, Jan, Paige Tolbert, Carol Rubin, Louis Guillette, and Richard Jackson. "Reproductive Toxins and Alligator Abnormalities at Lake Apopka, Florida." *Environmental Health Perspectives* 105 (1997): 1030–32.

Slavitt, David. "Day Sailing." In *Day Sailing,* 4. Chapel Hill: University of North Carolina Press, 1969.

Steinberg, Rafael. *Pacific and Southwest Asian Cooking.* New York: Time-Life, 1970.

Thoreau, Henry David. "Walden," 1854. In *The Portable Thoreau,* rev. ed. New York: Viking Press, 1964.

Warner, William. *Beautiful Swimmers: Watermen, Crabs, and the Chesapeake Bay.* Boston: Little, Brown, 1976.

Welch, Gillian. "Acony Bell." From the album *Revival.* Almo Sounds, 1996.

White, John, and Paul Hulton. *America, 1585: The Complete Drawings of John White.* Chapel Hill: University of North Carolina Press, 1984.

Whitman, Walt. "After the Sea Ship." In *Leaves of Grass,* 215. Modern Library. New York: Random House, 1891.

———. "In Cabin'd Ships at Sea." In *Leaves of Grass,* 4. Modern Library. New York: Random House, 1891.

Wolfe, Thomas. *Of Time and the River.* Scribner Classics, 1999.

Wordsworth, William. "To a Child." In *Selected Poetry,* 674. Edited by M. V. Doren. Modern Library. New York: Random House, 1950.

Index

Jennifer Frick-Ruppert is professor of biology and environmental science at Brevard College in western North Carolina. She earned her Ph.D. at Clemson University studying the developmental biology of a sea cucumber and performed further research on marine animals as a postdoctoral Fellow at the Smithsonian Marine Station in Fort Pierce, Florida. Her first book, *Mountain Nature: A Seasonal Natural History of the Southern Appalachians*, is a nonfiction work about biodiversity that was written for a popular audience. Jennifer and Edward Ruppert, who is a coauthor of *Seashore Animals of the Southeast* and the textbook *Invertebrate Zoology*, cruised aboard *Velella* for six years. They now own a Nor'Sea-27 named *Clio* that, together with their son, Fritz, they enjoy sailing on the waters of eastern North Carolina.

The University Press of Florida is the scholarly publishing agency for the State University System of Florida, comprising Florida A&M University, Florida Atlantic University, Florida Gulf Coast University, Florida International University, Florida State University, New College of Florida, University of Central Florida, University of Florida, University of North Florida, University of South Florida, and University of West Florida.